POETRIES
and
SCIENCES

Other Books by I. A. Richards

POETRIES
and
SCIENCES

A REISSUE OF SCIENCE AND POETRY

(1926, 1935) WITH COMMENTARY

I. A. RICHARDS, C.H.

———————————

W · W · NORTON & COMPANY · INC ·
NEW YORK

SBN 393 04308 8

1 2 3 4 5 6 7 8 9 0

CONTENTS

PREFACE

THIS LITTLE BOOK has had varied treatment at my hands. Soon after its appearance I took a dislike to it without being very sure why. What seemed to me its best and most clearly stated points were, I found, understood in ways which turned them into indefensible nonsense. That was, I came to feel, what the opponents—some of them eminent—wanted them to be. Was not that why they misread? They would, for example, in spite of careful explanations, persist in taking pseudo-statements to be false statements. It was in vain that I would amplify the distinction, appealing to the dictionary and offering *pseudopods* and *pseudocarps* in illustration. They still clung devoutly to their muddle. They were, I should have realized, simply confirming my account. They were replying with pseudo-statements: with "forms of words whose scientific truth or falsity is irrelevant to the purpose in hand." I should have been reassured, not annoyed.

At all events, in 1935 I tinkered up a Second Edition, Revised and Enlarged. The tinkerings included rephrasings and the note on pseudo-statement from which I have just quoted and a brief Appendix on the words *Nature* and *Belief*. It is this Second Edition which is here reprinted. Not long afterwards, I came to the conclusion that these would-be clarifications were still ineffective, being addressed to minds which were looking elsewhere—in part because what I had hoped to make them pay attention to would have disturbed their routines overmuch. For a time I went on trying. Here, for example, from 1940 or 1941, is the opening of an Introduction intended for another rewriting. I have added in brackets rephrasings which would now (1970) seem to be preferable.

The question this little book in its earlier forms endeavoured to face—and, I fear, to answer—was: "How should we conceive Science and Poetry?" It was not: "What are they?" That is a foolish question unless it is taken as short for "How may we conceive them?" Science and Poetry are not just *there* waiting for us to sketch or describe them. Without doubt there are different things (or activities) called Science and other, equally different, things called Poetry. But for our purposes in this discussion, Science and Poetry are not just "the things usually so called." If we started by looking over these things and making [*trying to make*] an inventory we would find that the things called Science are a very mixed bag and the things called Poetry still more so. That super-lexicographic task would be interesting [*highly useful*] but it would be History. It would give an account of how men have named these things [*what things men have named with these words*]. But our task is to decide [*ask*] how we should conceive some of these things and record [*give grounds for*], if we can, our decisions [*choices*]. Then we can try to persuade others to conceive them so.

In this task there are no fixed agreed starting points and no definitive conclusions. We think in order to see better where we may be starting from and where going. And, moreover, this discussion has to be in a peculiar fashion *about itself*. For if we [*were to*] divide human discourse into Science and Poetry (as my title [*may be supposed to do*] did) then we ought to ask (as I may not have done clearly enough) "Which am I talking here?" In asking the sorts of questions about Science and Poetry here raised, I have to say, if I can, what I am doing and what sorts of answers, poetic or scientific [*or mixed*] I am attempting to give. And it may be well to say, at this outset, that the answers have to be poetic—though presented in a prosaic fashion. For this is a matter not of fact but of choice.

It is easy for me now to see that this attempt, and the 1935 version, were the offspring of *Practical Criticism* and *Interpretation in Teaching*—as the original *S & P* was a side-shoot from *Principles of Literary Criticism*. I can see too why I did not pursue it. Instead I let the book drop out of print. Except for detached sections which have appeared fairly often in anthologies and compendia, it has been virtually unavailable for over a quarter of a century.

Why disinter and re-edit it now? This is a question that over half its sentences ask me. They get a threefold answer: (1) Unobjectionable doctrine on its prime topics must, it seems likely, wait for wiser men. But meanwhile the topics, being momentous, deserve whatever discussion may help us to see why they must, by present techniques, be so hard to be fair about. (2) There may be some value in noting, as frankly as is tolerable, what sorts of changes can result from a rather long-continuing and self-critical concern with how we should talk about language and its workings. (3) Two eyes, two ears see and hear better than one. Hearing and vision, moreover, endlessly correct one another. A similar opportunity may be offered us in comparing and

combining what is apparent in more abstract matters
from a number of positions. And, conversely, it may
be instructive to attempt to divine the shift of position
from changes in how the familiar objects of our regard
may appear.

One such change I have tried to make prominent in
my revision of the title. Titles raise, and sometimes set-
tle, more than they can account for. The original *S & P*,
perhaps echoing Matthew Arnold, offered an opposi-
tion and, for some, almost staged a conflict; at the least
a separation. It lent itself to being taken as a piece of
the politics of theology.

The new title: *Ps & Ss*—fending off (1) *Poetry and
the Sciences* as well as (2) *The Poetries and the Sci-
ences* and taking its character partly from their rejec-
tion—pretends to improvement in modesty: the first
might suggest an originative essence or creative activity
and its dealings with, and in, a varied range of studies;
the second would seem to propose a survey of two
great genera and an ordering of their species: a task
incomparably more ambitious than is in view here. The
plurals of the new title may perhaps usefully redirect
attention on the one hand to the genres and on the
other hand to the differences and dissensions between
mathematical, statistical and empirical treatments. These
are marches along which some conflict, interferences
and confusion now seem to be developing. These may
be escalated as data processing advances. Plurals also dis-
courage quests for premature ultimates and for equally
premature solutions by definition: from both of which

aberrations the essay now under renewed examination will be found to have suffered. Let us accordingly lay aside Poetry and Science and use instead as many different concepts of poetries and of sciences as we find compassable and convenient.

Among my indebtednesses to The Center for Advanced Studies, Wesleyan University, Middletown, Connecticut, not least I count leisure in the winter of 1966–67 to re-examine this old essay and consider what to do about it. Obviously attempts to improve it could go on indefinitely. That I stop now is due to the interventions of other tasks.

I. A. R.

1970

Science and Poetry
(1926, 1935)

The future of poetry is immense, because in poetry, where it is worthy of its high destinies, our race, as time goes on, will find an ever surer and surer stay. There is not a creed which is not shaken, not an accredited dogma which is not shown to be questionable, not a received tradition which does not threaten to dissolve. Our religion has materialized itself in the fact, in the supposed fact; it has attached its emotion to the fact, and now the fact is failing it. But for poetry the idea is everything.—

MATTHEW ARNOLD

I. THE GENERAL SITUATION

In the hour of the Blue Bird and the Bristol
Bomber, his thoughts are appropriate to the
years of the Penny Farthing.

W. H. AUDEN, *The Dog Beneath the Skin*

MAN'S PROSPECTS are not at present so rosy that he can
neglect any means of improving them. He has recently
made a number of changes in his customs and ways of
life, partly with intention, partly by accident. These
changes are involving such widespread further changes
that the fairly near future is likely to see an almost
complete reorganization of our lives, in their intimate
aspects as much as in their public. Man himself is chang-
ing, together with his circumstances; he has changed in
the past, it is true, but never perhaps so swiftly. His
circumstances are not known to have ever changed so
much or so suddenly before, with psychological as well
as with economic, social and political dangers. This
suddenness threatens us. Some parts of human nature
resist change more than others. We risk disaster if some
of our customs change while others which should change
with them stay as they are.

Habits that have endured for many thousands of years are not easy to throw off—least of all when they are habits of thought, and when they do not come into open conflict with changing circumstances, or do not clearly involve us in loss or inconvenience. Yet the loss may be great without our knowing anything about it. Before 1590 no one knew how inconvenient were our natural habits of thought about the ways in which a stone may fall; yet the modern world began when Galileo discovered what really happens. Only persons thought to be crazy knew before 1800 that ordinary traditional ideas as to cleanliness are dangerously inadequate. The infant's average "expectation of life" has increased by about thirty years since Lister upset them. Nobody before Sir Ronald Ross knew what were the consequences of thinking about malaria in terms of influences and miasmas instead of in terms of mosquitoes. The Roman Empire might perhaps have still been flourishing if someone had found this out before A.D. 100.†

With such examples all about us we can no longer, in any department of life, so easily accept what was good enough for our fathers as good enough for ourselves, or for our children. We are forced to wonder whether our ideas, even upon subjects apparently of little importance, such as poetry, may not be missing the main point. It becomes indeed somewhat alarming to recognize, as we must, that our habits of thought remain, as regards most of our affairs, much as they were five thousand years ago. The Sciences are, of course, simply the exceptions to this rule. Outside the Sciences

—and the greater part of our thinking still goes on outside the Sciences—we think very much as our ancestors thought a hundred or two hundred generations ago. Certainly this is so as regards official views about poetry. Is it not possible that these are wrong, as wrong as most ideas of an equally hoary antiquity? Is it not possible that to the men of the future our life today will seem a continual, ceaseless disaster due only to our own stupidity, to the nervelessness with which we accept and transmit ideas which do not and never have applied to anything?

The average educated man is growing more conscious,† an extraordinary significant change. It is probably due to the fact that his life is becoming more complex, more intricate, his desires and needs more varied and more apt to conflict. And as he becomes more conscious he can no longer be content to drift in unreflecting obedience to custom. He is forced to reflect. And if reflection often takes the form of inconclusive worrying, that is no more than might be expected in view of the unparalleled difficulty of the task. To live reasonably is much more difficult today than it was in Dr. Johnson's time, and even then, as Boswell shows, it was difficult enough.

To live reasonably is not to live by reason alone—the mistake is easy, and if carried far, disastrous—but to live in a way of which reason, a clear, full sense of the whole situation, would approve. And the most important part of the whole situation, as always, is ourselves, our constitution as systems responsive to that in which we live. The more we learn about the physical world, about our bodies, for example, the more points we find at which our ordinary behaviour is out of accord with the facts, inapplicable, wasteful, disadvantageous, dangerous or absurd. Witness our habit of boiling our vegetables. We have still to learn how to feed ourselves satisfactorily. Similarly, the little that is yet known about the mind already shows that our ways of thinking and feeling about very many of the things with which we concern ourselves are out of accord with the facts. This is pre-eminently true of our ways of thinking and feeling about poetry. We think and talk in terms which merge and confound orders which must be distinguished. We attribute to ourselves and to things powers which neither we nor they possess. And equally we overlook or misuse powers which are all important to us.

Day by day, in recent years, man is getting more out of place in Nature—in the Nature which his ancient habits of thought formed for him. Where he is going to he does not yet know, he has not yet decided. As a consequence he finds life more and more bewildering, more and more difficult to live coherently. Thus he turns to consider himself, his own nature. For the first step towards a reasonable way of life is a better understanding of human nature.†

It has long been recognized that if only something could be done in psychology remotely comparable to what has been achieved in physics, practical consequences might be expected even more remarkable than any that the engineer can contrive.† The first positive steps in the science of the mind have been slow in coming, but already they are beginning to change man's whole outlook.

II. THE POETIC EXPERIENCE

O chestnut tree, great rooted blossomer,
Are you the leaf, the blossom or the bole?
O body swayed to music, O brightening glance,
How can we know the dancer from the dance?

w. b. yeats, The Tower

EXTRAORDINARY CLAIMS have often been made for poetry
—Matthew Arnold's words quoted at the head of this
book are an example—claims which very many people
are inclined to view with astonishment or with the smile
which tolerance gives to the enthusiast. Indeed, a more
representative modern view would be that the future
of poetry is *nil*. Peacock's conclusion in his *The Four
Ages of Poetry* finds a more general acceptance. "A
poet in our times is a semi-barbarian in a civilized com-
munity. He lives in the days that are past. . . . In what-
ever degree poetry is cultivated, it must necessarily be to
the neglect of some branch of useful study: and it is a
lamentable thing to see minds, capable of better things,
running to seed in the specious indolence of these empty,
aimless mockeries of intellectual exertion. Poetry was the
mental rattle that awakened the attention of intellect in

the infancy of civil society: but for the maturity of mind
to make a serious business of the playthings of its child-
hood, is as absurd as for a grown man to rub his gums
with coral, and cry to be charmed asleep by the jingle
of silver bells." And with more regret many others—
Keats was among them—have thought that the inevitable
effect of the advance of science would be to destroy the
possibility of poetry.

What is the truth in this matter? How is our estimate
of poetry going to be affected by science? And how will
poetry itself be influenced? The extreme importance
which has in the past been assigned to poetry is a fact
which must be accounted for whether we conclude that
it was rightly assigned or not, and whether we consider
that poetry will continue to be held in such esteem or
not. It indicates that the case for poetry, whether right
or wrong, is one which turns on momentous issues. We
shall not have dealt adequately with it unless we have
raised questions of great significance.

Very much toil has gone to the endeavour to explain
the high place of poetry in human affairs, with, on the
whole, few satisfactory or convincing results. This is not
surprising. For in order to show how poetry is important
it is first necessary to discover to some extent what it is.†
Until recently this preliminary task could only be very
incompletely carried out; the psychology of instinct and
emotion was too little advanced; and, moreover, the
over-simple assumptions natural in pre-scientific enquiry
definitely stood in the way. Neither the professional psy-
chologist, whose interest in poetry is frequently not in-

tense, nor the man of letters, who as a rule has no adequate ideas of the mind as a whole, has been equipped for the investigation. Both a passionate knowledge of poetry and a capacity for dispassionate psychological analysis are required if it is to be satisfactorily prosecuted.

It will be best to begin by asking, "What *kind of a thing*, in the widest sense, is poetry?" When we have answered this we shall be ready to ask, "How can we use and misuse it?" and, "What reasons are there for thinking it valuable?"

Let us take an experience, ten minutes of a person's life, and describe it in broad outline. It is now possible to indicate its general structure, to point out what is important in it, what trivial and accessory, which features depend upon which, how it has arisen, and how it is probably going to influence his future experience. There are, of course, wide gaps in this description, none the less it *is* at last possible to understand in general how the mind works in an experience, and what sort of stream of events the experience is.

A poem, let us say Wordsworth's "Westminster Bridge" sonnet, is such an experience, it is the experience the right kind of reader has when he peruses the verses. And the first step to an understanding of the place and future of poetry in human affairs is to see what the general structure of such an experience is. Let us begin by reading it very slowly, preferably aloud, giving every syllable time to make its full effect upon us. And let us read it experimentally, repeating it, varying our tone of

voice until we are satisfied that we have caught its
rhythm as well as we are able, and—whether our reading
is such as to please other people or not—that we our-
selves at least are certain how it should "go."

> Earth has not anything to show more fair:
> Dull would he be of soul who could pass by
> A sight so touching in its majesty:
> This City now doth, like a garment, wear
> The beauty of the morning: silent, bare,
> Ships, towers, domes, theatres and temples lie
> Open unto the fields, and to the sky,
> All bright and glittering in the smokeless air.
> Never did sun more beautifully steep
> In his first splendour valley, rock or hill;
> Ne'er saw I, never felt, a calm so deep!
> The river glideth at its own sweet will:
> Dear God! the very houses seem asleep;
> And all that mighty heart is lying still!

We may best make our analysis of the experience that
arises through reading these lines, from the surface in-
wards, to speak metaphorically. The surface is the im-
pression of the printed words on the retina. This sets up
an agitation which we must follow as it goes deeper and
deeper.

The first things to occur (if they do not, the rest of the
experience will be gravely inadequate) are the sound of
the words "in the mind's ear" and the feel of the words
imaginarily spoken.† These together give the *full body*,
as it were, to the words, and it is with the full bodies of
words that the poet works, not with their printed signs.
The full bodies reflect the whole meaning of the words
as the printed signs cannot. But many people lose nearly
everything in poetry through failure to develop this in-

dispensable and controlling reflection.

Next arise various pictures "in the mind's eye"; not of
words but of things for which the words stand; perhaps
of ships, perhaps of hills; and together with them, it may
be, other images of various sorts. Images of what it feels
like to stand leaning on the parapet of Westminster
Bridge. Perhaps that odd thing, an image of "silence."
But, unlike the image-bodies of the words themselves,
those other images of things are not vitally impor-
tant. Those who have them may very well think them
indispensable, and *for them* they may be necessary; but
other people may not require them at all. This is a point
at which differences between individual minds are very
marked.

Thence onwards the agitation which is the experience
divides into a major and a minor branch, though the two
streams have innumerable interconnections and influence
one another intimately. Indeed, it is only as an expositor's
artifice that we may speak of them as two streams.

The minor branch we may call the intellectual stream;
the other, which we may call the active, or emotional,
stream, is made up of the play of our interests.

The intellectual stream is comparatively easy to fol-
low; it follows itself, so to speak; but it is the less impor-
tant of the two. In poetry it matters only *as a means;* it
directs and excites the active stream. It is made up of
thoughts, which are not static little entities that bob up
into consciousness and down again out of it, but fluent
happenings, events, which refer or point to the things
the thoughts are "of."

This pointing to things is all that thoughts do. They appear to do much more—to copy or to create—which are our chief illusions. The realm of pure thought is not an autonomous state. Our thoughts are the servants of our interests, and even when they seem to rebel it is some among our interests which are in insurrection. Our thoughts are pointers and it is the other, the active, stream which deals with the things which thoughts point to.

Some people who read verse (they do not often read much of it), are so constituted that very little more happens than this intellectual stream of thoughts. It is perhaps superfluous to point out that they miss the real poem. To exaggerate this part of the experience, and give it too much importance on its own account, is a notable current tendency, and for many people explains why they do not read poetry.

The active branch is what really matters; for from it all the energy of the whole agitation comes. The thinking which goes on is somewhat like the play of an ingenious and invaluable "governor" run by but controlling the main machine.† Every experience is essentially some interest or group of interests swinging back to rest.

To understand what an interest is we should picture the mind as a system of very delicately poised balances, a system which so long as we are in health is constantly *growing*. Every situation we come into disturbs some of these balances to some degree. The ways in which they swing back to a new equipoise are the impulses with which we respond to the situation. And the chief balances in the system are our chief interests.

Suppose that we carry a magnetic compass about in the neighbourhood of powerful magnets. The needle waggles as we move and comes to rest pointing in a new direction whenever we stand still in a new position. Suppose that instead of a single compass we carry an arrangement of many magnetic needles, large and small, swung so that they influence one another, some able only to swing horizontally, others vertically, others hung freely.† As we move, the perturbations in this system will be very complicated. But for every position in which we place it there will be a final position of rest for all the needles into which they will in the end settle down, a general poise for the whole system. But even a slight displacement may set the whole assemblage of needles busily readjusting themselves.

One further complication. Suppose that while all the needles influence one another, some of them respond only to some of the outer magnets among which the system is moving. The reader can easily draw a diagram if his imagination needs a visual support.

The mind is not unlike such a system if we imagine it to be incredibly complex. The needles are our interests, varying in their *importance*—that is in the degree to which any movement they make involves movement in the other needles. Each new disequilibrium, which a shift of position, a fresh situation, entails, corresponds to a need; and the wagglings which ensue as the system rearranges itself are our responses, the impulses through which we seek to meet the need. Often the new poise is not found until long after the original disturbance. Thus states of strain can arise which last for years.

The child comes into the world as a comparatively simple arrangement. Few things affect him, comparatively speaking, and his responses also are few and simple. But he very quickly becomes more complicated. His recurrent needs for food and for various attentions are constantly setting all his needles swinging. Little by little separate needs become departmentalized, as it were, sub-systems are formed; hunger causes one set of responses, the sight of his toys another, loud noises yet another, and so on. But the sub-systems never become quite independent. So he grows up, becoming susceptible to ever more numerous and more delicate influences, and as he grows, so his world grows with him.

He becomes more discriminating in some respects, he is thrown out of equilibrium by slighter differences in his situation. In other respects he becomes more stable. From time to time, through growth, fresh interests develop; sex is the outstanding example. His needs increase, he becomes capable of being upset by quite new causes, he becomes responsive to quite new aspects of the situation.

This development takes a very indirect course.† It would be still more erratic if society did not mould and remould him at every stage, reorganizing him incompletely two or three times over before he grows up. He reaches maturity in the form of a vast assemblage of major and minor interests, partly a chaos, partly a system, with some tracts of his personality fully developed and free to respond, others tangled and jammed in all kinds of accidental ways. It is this incredibly complex assemblage of interests to which the printed poem has to appeal. Sometimes the poem is itself the influence which disturbs us, sometimes it is merely a means by which already existing disturbances can right themselves. More usually perhaps it is both at once.

We must picture then the stream of the poetic experience as the swinging back into equilibrium of these disturbed interests. We are reading the poem in the first place only because we are in some way interested in doing so, only because some interest is attempting, directly or indirectly, to regain its poise thereby. And whatever happens as we read happens only for a similar reason. We understand the words (the intellectual branch of the stream goes on its way successfully) only because interests are reacting through that means. Our interpretation of the poem is the movement in these interests. All the rest of the experience is equally but more evidently our adaptation working itself out.

The rest of the experience is made up of emotions and attitudes. Emotions are what the reaction, with its reverberation in bodily changes, feels like. Attitudes [1] are the impulses towards one kind of behaviour or another which are set ready by the response. They are, as it were, its outward going part, though they may go no further than a provisional setting for occasions which never arise. Sometimes, as here in "Westminster Bridge,"

[1] For a further discussion of attitudes see the author's *Principles of Literary Criticism*, Chapter XV (Harcourt, Brace & World, Inc., 1925, 1968).

they are very easily overlooked. But consider a simpler case—a fit of laughter which it is absolutely essential to conceal, in church or during a solemn interview, for example. You contrive not to laugh; but there is no doubt about the activity of the impulses in their restricted form. The much more subtle and elaborate impulses which a poem excites are not different in principle. They do not show themselves as a rule, they do not come out into the open, largely because they are so complex. When they have adjusted themselves to one another and become organized into a coherent whole, the needs concerned may be satisfied. *In a fully developed man a state of readiness for action will take the place of action when the full appropriate situation for action is not present.* An essential peculiarity of poetry as of all the arts is that the full appropriate situation is *not* present. It is an *actor* we are seeing upon the stage, not Hamlet. So readiness for action takes the place of actual behaviour.

This is the main plan then of the experience. Signs on the retina, taken up by sets of needs (remember how many other impressions all day long remain entirely *unnoticed* because no interest responds to them), thence an elaborate agitation and reorganization, one branch of which is *thoughts of* what the words mean, the other an emotional response leading to the development of *attitudes*, preparations, that is, for actions which may or may not take place; the two branches being in intimate connection.

But though these attitudes may not, and usually will not, find direct outlets, recognizable as appropriate to them, this is not to say that they do not incessantly control all our intercourse with the world. When they are supposed not to do so, we have "art for art's sake" and a "barren aestheticism."

We must look now a little more closely at these connections. It may seem odd that we do not more definitely make the thoughts the rulers and causes of the rest of the response. To do just this has been in fact the grand error of traditional psychology. Man prefers to stress the features which distinguish him from monkey, and chief among these are his intellectual capacities. Important though they are, he has given them a rank to which they are not entitled. Intellect is an adjunct to the interests, a means by which they adjust themselves more successfully. And though his intellect is what is distinctive in man, he is not primarily an intelligence; he is a system of interests. Intelligence helps man but does not run him.

Partly through this natural mistake, and partly because intellectual operations are so much easier to study, the traditional analysis of the working of the mind has been turned upside down. It is largely as a remedy from the difficulties which this mistake involves that poetry may have so much importance in the future. But let us look again more closely at the poetic experience.

In the first place, why is it essential in reading poetry to give the words their full imagined sound and body? What is meant by saying that the poet works with this sound and body? The answer is that even before the words have been intellectually understood and the thoughts they occasion formed and followed, the movement and sound of the words is playing deeply and intimately upon the interests. How this happens is a matter which has yet to be successfully investigated, but that it happens no sensitive reader of poetry doubts. A good deal of poetry and even some great poetry exists (*e.g.*, some of Shakespeare's songs and, in a different way, much of the best of Swinburne) in which the sense of the words can be *almost* entirely missed or neglected without loss.† Never, perhaps, entirely without effort, however; though sometimes with advantage. But the plain fact that the relative importance of grasping the sense of the words may vary (compare Browning's "Before" with his "After") is enough for our purpose here.

In nearly all poetry the sound and feel of the words, what is often called the *form* of the poem in opposition to its *content*, get to work first, and the senses in which the words are later more explicitly taken are subtly influenced by this fact. Most words are ambiguous as regards their plain sense, especially in poetry. We can take them as we please in a variety of senses. The senses we are pleased to choose are those which most suit the impulses already stirring and giving form to the verse. Thus the form often seems an inexplicable premonition of a meaning which we have not yet grasped. The same thing can be noticed in conversation. Not the strict logical sense of what is said, but the tone of voice and the occasion are the primary factors by which we interpret. Science, it is worth noting, endeavours with increasing success to bar out these factors. We believe a scientist because he can substantiate his remarks, not because he is eloquent or forcible in his enunciation. In fact, we distrust him when he seems to be influencing us by his manner.

In its use of words most poetry is the reverse of science. Very definite thoughts do occur, but not because the words are so chosen as logically to bar out all possibilities but one. They are not; but the manner, the tone of voice, the cadence and the rhythm play upon our interests and make *them* pick out from among an indefinite number of possibilities the precise particular thoughts which they need. This is why poetical descriptions often seem so much more accurate than prose descriptions. Language logically and scientifically used cannot describe a landscape or a face. To do so it would need a prodigious apparatus of names for shades and nuances, for precise particular qualities. These names do not exist, so other means have to be used. The poet, even when, like Ruskin or De Quincey, he writes in prose, makes the reader pick out the precise particular senses required from an indefinite number of possible senses which a word, phrase or sentence may carry. The means by which he does this are many and varied. Some of them have been mentioned above, but the way in which he uses them is the poet's own secret, something which cannot be taught. He knows how to do it, but he does not himself necessarily know how it is done.

Misunderstanding and under-estimation of poetry are mainly due to over-insistence on the thought in separation from the rest. We can see still more clearly that thought is not the prime factor if we consider for a

moment not the experience of the reader but that of
the poet. Why does the poet use these words and no
others? Not because they stand for a series of thoughts
which in themselves are what he is concerned to com-
municate. It is never what a poem *says* which matters,
but what it *is*. The poet is not writing as a scientist. He
uses these words because the interests whose movement
is the growth of the poem combine to bring them, just
in this form, into his consciousness *as a means of order-
ing, controlling and consolidating* the uttered experience
of which they are themselves a main part. The experi-
ence itself, the tide of impulses sweeping through the
mind, is the source and the sanction of the words. They
represent this experience itself, not any set of percep-
tions or reflections, though often to a reader who ap-
proaches the poem wrongly they will seem to be only
a series of remarks about other things. But to a suitable
reader the words—if they actually spring from experi-
ence and are not due to verbal habits, to the desire to
be effective, to factitious excogitation, to imitation, to
irrelevant contrivances, or to any other of the failings
which prevent most people from writing poetry—the
words will reproduce in his mind a similar play of in-
terests putting him for the while into a similar situation
and leading to the same response.†

Why this should happen is the mystery of com-
munication. An inconceivably intricate concourse of
impulses brings the words together. Then in another
mind the affair in part reverses itself, the words bring
into being an analogous concourse of impulses. The

words which seem to be the effect of the experience in
the first instance, seem to become the cause of a simi-
lar experience in the second. A very odd thing to hap-
pen, not exactly paralleled outside communication. But
this description is not quite accurate. The words, as
we have seen, are not simply the effect in one case,
nor the cause in the other. In both cases they are the
part of the experience which binds it together, which
gives it a definite structure and keeps it from being a
mere welter of disconnected impulses. They are *the
key*, to borrow a useful metaphor from McDougall, for
this particular combination of impulses. So regarded it
is less strange that what the poet wrote should repro-
duce a relevant experience in the mind of the reader.
But no train of reflection could make us more aware
of the dependence of poetry upon a continuity (which
need not be constancy) in language.

III. WHAT IS VALUABLE

No longer in Lethean foliage caught
Begin the preparation for your death
And from the fortieth winter by that thought
Test every work of intellect or faith.

w. b. yeats, The Winding Stair

ENOUGH PERHAPS as to the kind of thing a poem is. Let us now turn to the further questions, "Of what use is it?" "Why and how is it valuable?" for which the first point to be made is that poetic experiences are valuable (when they are) in the same ways [1] as any other experiences. They are to be judged by the same standards. What are these?

Extraordinarily diverse views have been held upon this point. Very naturally, since such very different ideas have been entertained as to what kind of thing an experience is. For our opinions as to the differences between good and bad experiences depend inevitably upon what we take an experience to be. As fashions have changed in psychology men's ethical theories have

---

1. How deep are the "ways" we select for consideration is of course what is decided here.

followed suit. When a created, simple and eternal soul was the pivotal point, Good was conformity with the will of the Creator, Evil was rebellion. When the associationist psychologists substituted a swarm of sensations and images for the soul, Good became pleasure and Evil became pain, and so on. A long chapter of the history of opinions has still to be written tracing these changes. When the mind is taken to be an organic hierarchy of interests, what will be the difference between Good and Evil?

For this account it will be the difference between free and wasteful organization, between fullness and narrowness of life. For if the mind is a system of interests, and if an experience is their movement, the worth of any experience is a matter of the degree to which the mind, through this movement, proceeds towards a wider equilibrium.

This is a first approximation. It needs qualifying and expanding if it is to become a satisfactory theory. Let us see how some of these amendments would run.

Consider an hour of any person's life. It holds out innumerable possibilities. Which of these are realized depends upon two main groups of factors: the external situation in which he is and has been living, his surroundings, including the other people with whom he is in contact; and secondly, his psychological make-up. The first of these, the external situation, may be given too much importance, though not in politics. Biologists have recently been reminding us that organism and environment are not independent terms and we have only

to notice what very different experiences different people undergo when in closely similar situations to agree.†
A situation which is dullness itself for one may be full of excitement for another. What an individual responds to is not the whole situation but a selection from it, and as a rule few people make the same selection. What is selected, and thus the relevant environment, is decided by the organization of the individual's interests.

Now let us simplify the case by supposing that nothing which happens during this hour is going to have any further consequences either in our hypothetical person's life or in anyone else's. He is going to cease to exist when the clock strikes—but for our purposes he must be imagined not to know this—and no one is to be a whit the better or worse whatever he thinks, feels or does during the hour. What shall we say it would be best for him, if he could, to do?

We need not bother to imagine the detail of the external situation or the character of the man. We can answer our question in general terms without doing so. The man has a certain definite instinctive and acquired make-up—the result of his past history, including his heredity. There will be many things which he cannot do which another man could, and many things which he cannot do in this situation, whatever it is, which he could do in other situations. But given this particular man in this particular situation, our question is, which of the possibilities open to him would be better than which others? How would we, as friendly observers, like to see him living?

Setting pain aside, we may perhaps agree that torpor would be the worst choice. Complete inertness, lifelessness, would be the sorriest spectacle—anticipating too nearly and unnecessarily what is to happen when the hour strikes.† We can then perhaps agree, though here more resistance from preconceived ideas may be encountered, that the best choice would be the opposite of torpor, that is to say, the fullest, keenest, most active and completest kind of life.

Such a life is one which brings into play as many as possible of the *positive* interests. We can leave out the negative interests. It would be a pity for our friend to be frightened or disgusted even for a minute of his precious hour.

But this is not all. It is not enough that many interests should be stirred. There is a more important point to be noted.

> The Gods approve
> The depth and not the tumult of the soul.

The interests must come into play and remain in play with as little conflict among themselves as possible. In other words, the experience must be organized so as to give all the impulses of which it is composed the greatest possible degree of freedom.[2]

It is in this respect that people differ most from one another. It is this which separates the good life from the bad. Far more life is wasted through muddled mental organization than through lack of opportunity. Con-

2. See *The Foundations of Aesthetics*, by C. K. Ogden, James Wood and the author, pp. 74 ff. for a description of such experience.

flicts between different impulses, when they are not a
necessary mode of the rectification of the mind, are, as
the alienist knows, the greatest evils which afflict man-
kind.

The best life then which we can wish for our friend
will be one in which as much as possible of himself is
engaged. And this with as little conflict, as little frus-
trating interference between different sub-systems of
his activities as there can be. The more he lives and
the less he thwarts himself the better. That briefly is
our answer as outside observers abstractly describing
the state of affairs. And if it is asked, what does such
life feel like, how is it to live through? the answer is
that it feels like and is the experience of poetry.

There are two ways in which conflict can be avoided
or overcome. By conquest and by conciliation. One or
other of the contesting impulses can be suppressed, or
they can come to a mutual arrangement, they can ad-
just themselves to one another. We owe to psychoanal-
ysis enough evidence as to the extreme difficulty of sup-
pressing any vigorous impulse. When it seems to be
suppressed it is often found to be really as active as
ever, but in some other form, generally a troublesome
one. Persistent mental imbalances are the source of
nearly all our troubles. For this reason, as well as for
the simpler reason that suppression is wasteful of life,
conciliation is always to be preferred to conquest. Peo-
ple who are always winning victories over themselves
might equally well be described as always enslaving

themselves.† Their lives become unnecessarily narrow.

Unfortunately, most of us, left to ourselves, have no option but to go in for extensive attempts at self-conquest. It is our only means of escape from chaos. Our impulses must have some order, some organization, or we do not live ten minutes without disaster. In the past, Tradition, a kind of Treaty of Versailles assigning frontiers and spheres of influence to the different interests, and based chiefly upon conquest, ordered our lives in a moderately satisfactory manner. But Tradition is weakening. Moral authorities are not as well backed by beliefs as they were; their sanctions are declining in force. We are in need of something to take the place of the old order. Not in need of a new balance of power, a new arrangement of conquests, but of a League of Nations for the moral ordering of the impulses; a new order based on conciliation, not on attempted suppression.

Only the rarest individuals hitherto have achieved such an order, and never without disorganization of the ordinary social life. We may think of Blake. But many have achieved it for a brief while, for particular phases of experience, and many have recorded it for these phases.

Of these records poetry consists.

But before going on to this new point let us return for a moment to our hypothetical friend who is enjoying his last hour, and suppose this limitation removed. Instead of such an hour let us consider any hour, one which has consequences for his future and for other people. Let us consider any piece of any life. How far is our argument affected? Will our standards of good and evil be altered?

Clearly the case now is, in certain respects, different; it is much more complicated. We have to take these consequences into account. We have to regard his experience not in itself alone, but as a piece of his life and as a factor in other people's situations. We have to recognize that man is a social being, that only by a dehumanizing fiction do we regard him as an individual, and thus that moral questions put in such terms contain a contradiction. If we are to approve of the experience, it must not only be full of life and free from conflict, but it must be likely to lead to other experiences, both his own and those of other people, also full of life and free from conflict. And often, in actual fact, it has to be less full of life and more restricted than it might be in order to protect such futures. A momentary individual good has often to be sacrificed for the sake of a later or a general good. Conflicts are often necessary in order that they should not occur later. The mutual adjustment of conflicting impulses may take time, and an acute struggle may be the only way in which they can learn to co-operate peacefully in the future, and transform themselves into a more integrated way of life.

But all these complications and qualifications do not disturb the conclusion we arrived at through considering the simpler case. A good experience is still one full of life, in the sense explained, or derivatively one conducive to experiences full of life. An evil experience is one which is self-thwarting or conducive to stultifying conflicts. So far then, all is sound and shipshape in the argument, and we can go on to consider the poet.

IV. THE COMMAND OF LIFE

Eyes, ears, tongue, nostrils bring
News of revolt, inadequate counsel to
An infirm king.

w. h. auden, *Paid on Both Sides*

THE CHIEF CHARACTERISTIC OF poets is their amazing
command of words. This is not a mere matter of vo-
cabulary, though it is significant that Shakespeare's vo-
cabulary is the richest and most varied that any English
poet has ever used. It is not the quantity of words a
writer has at his disposal but the way in which he dis-
poses them that gives him his rank as a poet. His sense
of how they modify one another, how their separate
effects in the mind combine, how they fit into the whole
response, is what matters. As a rule the poet is not con-
scious of the reasons why just these words and no others
best serve. They fall into their place without his con-
scious control, and a feeling of rightness, of inevitability,
is commonly his sole conscious ground for his certainty
that he has ordered them aright. It would as a rule be
idle to ask him why he used a particular rhythm or a

particular epithet.† He might give reasons, but they would probably be mere rationalizations having nothing to do with the matter. For the choice of the rhythm or the epithet was not an intellectual, that is, an analysable, matter (though it may be capable of an intellectual justification), but was a movement of interest seeking to confirm itself, or to order itself with its fellows.

It is very important to realize how deep are the motives which govern the poet's use of words. No study of other poets which is not an impassioned study will help him. He can learn much from other poets, but only by letting them influence him deeply, not by any superficial examination of their "style." For the motives which shape a poem spring from the root of the mind. The poet's style is the direct outcome of the way in which his interests are organized. That amazing capacity of his for ordering speech is only a part of a more amazing capacity for ordering his experience.

This is the explanation of the fact that poetry cannot be written by cunning and study, by craft and contrivance. To a superficial glance the productions of the mere scholar, steeped in the poetry of the past and animated by intense emulation and a passionate desire to place himself among the poets, will often look extraordinarily like poetry. His words may seem as subtly and delicately ordered as words can be, his epithets as happy, his transitions as daring, his simplicity as perfect. By every intellectual test he may succeed. But unless the ordering of the words sprang, not from knowledge of the technique of poetry added to a desire to write some, but from an actual supreme ordering of *experience*, a closer approach to his work will betray it. Characteristically its rhythm will give it away. For rhythm is no matter of tricks with syllables, but directly reflects personality. It is not separable from the words to which it belongs. Moving rhythm in poetry arises only from genuinely stirred impulses, and is a more subtle index than any other to the order of the interests.

Poetry, in other words, cannot be imitated; it cannot be faked so as to baffle the only test that ought ever to be applied. It is unfortunately true that this test is often very difficult to apply. And to be sure that the test has been applied is always hazardous. For the test is this—that only genuine poetry will give to the reader who approaches it in the proper manner a response which is as passionate, noble and serene as the experience of the poet, the master of speech, because in the creative moment he is the master of experience itself. "Passionate," "noble," "serene" preserve themselves from misuse no better than other words; we can rely upon none of them and even less upon any other *criterion* of the omniform self-completing motions of the mind. If it is so, it will prove itself—but not necessarily to us or at once. And apart from this, it is easy to read carelessly and shallowly, and easy to mistake for the response something which does not properly belong to it at all. By careless reading we miss what is in the poem. And in some states of mind—for example, when intoxicated—the silliest doggerel may seem sublime. What happened was not due to the doggerel but to the drink.

With these general considerations in mind we may turn now from the question—What can the dawning science of psychology tell us about poetry?—to the allied questions—How is science in general, and the new outlook upon the world which it induces, already affecting poetry, and to what extent may science make obsolete the poetry of the past? To answer these questions we need to sketch some of the changes which have recently come about in our world picture, and to consider anew what it is that we demand from poetry.

V. THE NEUTRALIZATION
OF NATURE

All those large dreams by which men long live
   well
Are magic-lanterned on the smoke of hell;
  This then is real, I have implied,
  A painted, small, transparent slide.

WILLIAM EMPSON

POETRY IS FAILING US, or we it, if after our reading we do not find ourselves changed; not with a temporary change, such as luncheon or slumber will produce, from which we inevitably work back to the *status quo ante*, but with a permanent alteration of our possibilities as responsive individuals in good or bad adjustment to an all but overwhelming concourse of stimulations. How much contemporary poetry has the power to make such deep changes? Let us set aside youthful enthusiasms; there is a time in most lives when, rightly enough, Mr. Masefield, Mr. Kipling, Mr. Drinkwater, or even Mr. Noyes or Mr. Studdert Kennedy may profoundly affect the awakening mind; it is being introduced to poetry, or rather to the possibility [1] of emotional experience instigated, if not wholly controlled, through ordered words. Later on, looking back, we can see that any one of a hundred other poets would have served as well. Let us consider only the experienced reader, shaped by and responsive to a wide variety of the pressures from the contemporary situation, and familiar also with many different modes of the poetry of the past.

Contemporary poetry which will, accidents apart, modify the attitudes of this reader will be such as would not have been written in another age than our own. It will have sprung in part from the contemporary situation. It will be the outgrowth of needs, impulses, attitudes, which did not arise in the same form for poets in the past. And correspondingly—though this we are less willing to acknowledge—the poetry of the past will be read by such a reader in new ways. "The eye altering alters all." A poem no more than any other object is independent of the interests by which it is apprehended. Our attitudes to man, to nature, and to the universe which contains them both change with every generation, and have changed more extensively and more deeply in recent years. We cannot leave these changes out of account in speculating about modern poetry, though, of course, arguments from them are no valid ground for appraisal. When attitudes are changing neither criticism nor poetry remains stationary. To

1. See the admirable and important *Note on the development of taste in poetry* at the end of Chapter I of Mr. Eliot's *The Use of Poetry* (Barnes & Noble, Inc., 1955).

those who realize what the poet is this will be obvious; all literary history bears it out.

It would be of little use to give a list of the chief recent intellectual revolutions and to attempt to deduce therefrom what must be happening to poetry. The effects upon our attitudes of changes of opinion are too complex to be calculated so. What we have to consider is not men's current opinions but their attitudes—how they feel about this or that as part of the world; what relative importance its different aspects have for them; what they are prepared to sacrifice for what; what they trust, what they are frightened by, what they desire. To discover these things we must go to the poets. Unless they are failing us, they will show us just these things.

They will *show* them, but, of course, they will not state them. Their poetry will not be *about* their attitudes in the sense in which a treatise on anatomy is about the structure of the body. It arises out of attitudes and will evoke them in an adequate reader, but, as a rule, it will not mention any. And when it does they may be entering dramatically only as means. We must, of course, expect occasional essays in verse upon psychological topics, but these should not mislead us. Most of the attitudes with which poetry is concerned are indescribable for reasons suggested in Section Two above—and can only be named or spoken about indirectly through the situations (typically poems) which evoke them. The poem, the actual experience as it forms itself in the mind of the fit reader, controlling his responses to the world and ordering his impulses, does not ordinarily speak about its purposes. It has no need to while it can effect them. Poetry is thus our best evidence as to how other men feel about things; and as we read it, we discover not so much how life seems to another, as how it is for ourselves.

Although we cannot describe attitudes in terms which do not apply also to others which we are not considering, and although we cannot deduce a poet's attitudes from the general intellectual background, none the less, after reading his poetry, when his experience has induced our own, we can sometimes profitably look round us to see why these attitudes should be so very different, in some ways, from those we find in the poetry of one hundred or of one thousand years ago. In so doing we gain a means of indicating what these attitudes are, useful both for those who are constitutionally unable to read poetry (an increasing number), and for those victims of education who neglect modern poetry because they "don't know what to make of it."

What, then, has been happening to the intellectual background, to the world-picture, and in what ways may changes here have caused a reorganization of our attitudes?

The central dominant change may be described as the *Neutralization of Nature*,[2] the transference from the Magical View of the world to the scientific, a change so great that it is perhaps only paralleled historically by the change, from whatever adumbration of a world-pic-

2. See Appendix.

ture preceded the Magical View, to the Magical View itself. By the Magical View I mean, roughly, the belief in a world of spirits and powers which control events, and which can be evoked and, to some extent, controlled themselves by human practices. The belief in inspiration and the beliefs underlying ritual are representative parts of this view. It has been decaying slowly for some three hundred years, but its definite overthrow has taken place only in the last seventy.† Vestiges and survivals of it prompt and direct a great part of our daily affairs, but it is no longer the world-picture which an informed mind most easily accepts. There is some evidence that poetry, together with the other arts, arose with this Magical View. It is a possibility to be seriously considered that poetry may pass away with it.

The reasons for the downfall of the Magical View are familiar. It seems to have arisen as a consequence of an increase in man's knowledge of and command over nature (the discovery of agriculture). It fell through the extension of that knowledge of and command over nature. Throughout its (ten thousand years?) reign its stability has been due to its capacity for satisfying men's emotional needs through its adequacy as an object for their attitudes. We must remember that human attitudes have developed always *inside* the social group; they are what a man feels, the mainsprings of his behavior towards his fellow-men, and their application to the inhuman is an extension by metaphor. Thus the Magical View, being an interpretation of nature in terms of man's own most intimate and most important affairs, suits man's emotional make-up better than any other view possibly can. The attraction of the Magical View lay very little in the actual command over nature which it gave. That Galton was the first person to test the efficacy of prayer experimentally is an indication of this. What did give the Magical View its standing was the ease and adequacy with which the universe therein presented could be emotionally handled, the scope offered for man's love and hatred, for his terror as well as for his hope and his despair. It gave life a shape, a sharpness, and a coherence that no other means could so easily secure.

In its place we have the universe of the mathematician, a field for the tracing out of ever wider and more general uniformities. A field in which intellectual certainty is available, on an unlimited scale. Also the despondencies, the emotional excitements accompanying research and discovery, again on an unprecedented scale. Thus a number of men who might in other times have been poets may today be in biochemical laboratories—a fact of which we might avail ourselves, did we feel the need, in defence of an alleged present poverty in poetry. But apart from these thrills, what has the world-picture of science to do with human emotions? A god voluntarily or involuntarily subject to the General Theory of Relativity does not make an emotional appeal. So this form of compromise fails. Various emergent deities have been suggested—by Mr. Wells, by Professors Alexander and Lloyd Morgan—

but, alas! the reasons for suggesting them have become too clear and conscious. They are there to meet a demand, not to make one; they do not do the work for which they were invented.

The revolution brought about by science is, in short, too drastic to be met by any such half-measures. It touches the central principle by which the mind has been deliberately organized in the past, and no alteration in beliefs,[3] however great, will restore equilibrium while that principle is retained. I come now to the main purport of these remarks.

Ever since man first grew self-conscious and reflective he has supposed that his feelings, his attitudes, and his conduct spring from his knowledge. That as far as he could it would be wise for him to organize himself in this way, with knowledge[4] as the foundation on which should rest feeling, attitude and behavior. In point of fact, he never has been so organized, knowledge having been until recently too scarce; but he has constantly been persuaded that he was built on this plan, and has endeavoured to carry the structure further on these lines. He has sought for knowledge, supposing that it would itself *directly* excite a right orientation to existence, supposing that, if he only knew what the world was like, this knowledge in itself would show

3. See Appendix.
4. *I.e.*, thoughts which are both true and evidenced, in the narrower stricter senses. For a discussion of some relevant senses of "truth" and "knowledge" see *Principles of Literary Criticism*, Chapters XXXIII and XXXIV, and *Mencius on the Mind*, Chapter IV, also *The Meaning of Meaning* (with C. K. Ogden; Harcourt, Brace & World, Inc., 1923, 1959), Chapters VII and X.†

him how to feel towards it, what attitudes to adopt, and with what aims to live. He has constantly called what he found in this quest "knowledge," unaware that it was hardly ever pure, unaware that his feelings, attitudes and behaviour were *already* oriented by his physiological and social needs, and were themselves, for the most part, the sources of whatever it was that he supposed himself to be knowing.

Suddenly, not long ago, he began to get genuine knowledge on a large scale—knowledge, that is to say, purified from the influences of his wishes or his fears. The process went faster and faster; it snowballed. Now he has to face the fact that the edifices of supposed knowledge, with which he so long buttressed and supported his attitudes, will no longer stand up, and, at the same time, he has to recognise that pure knowledge is irrelevant to his aims, that it has no *direct* bearing upon what he should feel, or what he should attempt to do.

For science, as our most elaborate way of *pointing* to things systematically, tells us and can tell us nothing about the nature of things in any *ultimate* sense. It can never answer any question of the form: *What* is so and so? It can only tell us *how* such and such behaves. And it does not attempt to do more than this. Nor, indeed, can more than this be done. Those ancient, deeply troubling formulations that begin with "What" and "Why" —as contrasted with "How"—prove, when we examine them, to be not questions at all; but requests—for emotional satisfaction. They indicate our desire not for knowledge, the indifferent and emotionally neutral knowledge which is yielded by science, but for assurance [5], a point which appears clearly when we look into the "How" of questions and requests, of knowledge and desire. Science can tell us about man's place in the universe and his chances; that the place is precarious, and the chances problematical. It can enormously increase our chances if we can make wise use of it. But it cannot tell us what we are or what this world is; not because these are insoluble questions, but because they are not scientific questions at all. Science cannot answer these pseudo-questions; they do not belong to its province. Nor can philosophy or religion "answer" them in the sense in which science has taught us to expect answers to its questions. As the senses of "question" shift so do those of "answer" and those of "fact," "truth," "belief" and "knowledge" with them. The new prestige and power of science which are due to its separation from confusion with other modes of inquiry are shifting these senses and forcing a more general awareness of their differences upon us. And, with that, all the varied "answers" which have for ages been regarded as the keys of wisdom are, for many minds, in danger of dissolving together.

The result is a biological crisis which is not likely to be decided without trouble. It is one which we can, perhaps, decide for ourselves, partly by thinking, partly

5. On this point the study of the child's questions included in *The Language and Thought of the Child* by J. Piaget (Humanities Press, Inc., third edition, 1959), is illuminating.†

by reorganizing our minds in other ways; otherwise it may be decided for us, not in the way we should choose. While it lasts it puts a strain on each individual and upon society, which is part of the explanation of many modern difficulties, the difficulties of the poet in particular, to come back to our present subject. I have not really been far away.

VI. POETRY AND BELIEFS

Control of the passes was, he saw, the Key
To this new district, but who would get it?
He, the trained spy, had walked into the trap
For a bogus guide, seduced with the old tricks.

W. H. AUDEN

THE BUSINESS OF THE POET, as we have seen, is to give
order and coherence, and so freedom, to a body of
experience. To do so through words which act as its
skeleton, as a structure by which the impulses which
make up the experience are adjusted to one another and
act together. The means by which words do this are
many and varied. To work them out is a problem for
linguistic psychology, that embarrassed young heir to
philosophy.† What little can be done shows already
that most critical dogmas of the past are either false or
nonsense. A little knowledge is not here a danger, but
clears the air in a remarkable way.

Roughly and inadequately, even in the dim light of
present knowledge, we can say that words work in the
poem in two main fashions: as sensory stimuli and as
(in the *widest* sense) symbols.‡ We must refrain from

considering the sensory side of the poem, remarking only that it is *not* in the least independent of the other side, and that it has for definite reasons prior importance in most poetry. We must confine ourselves to the other function of words in the poem, or rather, omitting much that is of secondary relevance, to one form of that function, let me call it *pseudo-statement*.†

It will be admitted—by those who distinguish between scientific statement, where truth is ultimately a matter of verification as this is understood in the laboratory, and emotive utterance, where "truth" is primarily acceptability *by* some attitude, and more remotely is the acceptability *of* this attitude itself—that it is *not* the poet's business to make scientific statements. Yet poetry has constantly the air of making statements, and important ones; which is one reason why some mathematicians cannot read it. They find the alleged statements to be *false*. It will be agreed that their approach to poetry and their expectations from it are mistaken. But what exactly is the other, the right, the poetic, approach and how does it differ from the mathematical?

The poetic approach evidently limits the framework of possible consequences into which the pseudo-statement is taken. For the scientific approach this framework is unlimited. Any and every consequence is relevant. If any of the consequences of a statement conflicts with acknowledged fact then so much the worse for the statement. Not so with the pseudo-statement when poetically approached. The problem is—just how does

the limitation work? One tempting account is in terms
of a supposed universe of discourse, a world of make-
believe, of imagination, of recognized fictions common
to the poet and his readers. A pseudo-statement which
fits into this system of assumptions would be regarded
as "poetically true"; one which does not, as "poetically
false." This attempt to treat "poetic truth" on the model
of general "coherence theories" is very natural for cer-
tain schools of logicians but is inadequate, on the wrong
lines from the outset. To mention two objections, out
of many; there is no means of discovering what the
"universe of discourse" is on any occasion, and the kind
of coherence which must hold within it, supposing it
to be discoverable, is not an affair of logical relations.
Attempt to define the system of propositions into which

O Rose, thou art sick!

must fit, and the logical relations which must hold be-
tween them if it is to be "poetically true"; the absurdity
of the theory becomes evident.

We must look further. In the poetic approach the
relevant consequences are not logical or to be arrived
at by a partial relaxation of logic. Except occasionally
and by accident logic does not enter at all. The rele-
vant consequences are those which arise through our
emotional organization. The acceptance which a pseudo-
statement receives is entirely governed by its effects
upon our feelings and attitudes. Logic only comes in,
if at all, in subordination, as a servant to our emotional
response. It is an unruly servant, however, as poets and

readers are constantly discovering. A pseudo-statement is "true" if it suits and serves some attitude or links together attitudes which on other ground are desirable. This kind of "truth" is so opposed to scientific "truth" that it is a pity to use so similar a word, but at present it is difficult to avoid the malpractice.[1] †

This brief analysis may be sufficient to indicate the fundamental disparity and opposition between pseudo-statements as they occur in poetry and statements as they occur in science. A pseudo-statement is a form of words which is justified entirely by its effect in releasing or organizing our impulses and attitudes (due regard being had for the better or worse organizations of these *inter se*); a statement, on the other hand, is justified by its truth, *i.e.*, its correspondence, in a highly technical sense, with the fact to which it points.

Statements true and false alike do, of course, constantly touch off attitudes and action. Our daily practical existence is largely guided by them. On the whole true statements are of more service to us than false ones. None the less we do not and, at present, cannot order our emotions and attitudes by true statements alone. Nor is there any probability that we ever shall contrive to do so. This is one of the great new dangers to which civilization is exposed. Countless pseudo-statements— about God, about the universe, about human nature,

1. A pseudo-statement, as I use the term, is not necessarily false in any sense. It is merely a form of words whose scientific truth or falsity is irrelevant to the purpose in hand.
"Logic" in this paragraph is, of course, being used in a limited and conventional, or popular, sense.

the relations of mind to mind, about the soul, its rank and destiny—pseudo-statements which are pivotal points in the organization of the mind, vital to its well-being, have suddenly become, for sincere, honest and informed minds, impossible to believe as for centuries they have been believed.[2] The accustomed incidences of the modes of believing are changed irrecoverably; and the knowledge which has displaced them is not of a kind upon which an equally fine organization of the mind can be based.†

This is the contemporary situation. The remedy, since there is no prospect of our gaining adequate knowledge, and since indeed it is fairly clear that scientific knowledge cannot meet this need, is to cut our pseudo-statements free from that kind of belief which is appropriate to verified statements. So released they will be changed, of course, but they can still be the main instruments by which we order our attitudes to one another and to the world. This is not a desperate remedy, for, as poetry conclusively shows, even the most important among our attitudes can be aroused and maintained without any believing of a factual or

2. See Appendix. For the mind I am considering here the question "Do I believe *x?*" is no longer the same. Not only the "What" that is to be believed but the "How" of the believing has changed— through the segregation of science and its clarification of the techniques of proof. This is the danger; and the remedy suggested is a further differentiation of the "Hows." To these differences correspond differences in the senses of "is so" and "being" where, as is commonly the case, "is so" and "being" assert believings. As we admit this, the world that "is" divides into worlds incommensurable in respect of so called "degrees of reality." Yet, and this is all-important, these worlds have an order, with regard to one another, which is the order of the mind; and interference between them imperils sanity.

verifiable order entering in at all. We need no such beliefs, and indeed we must have none, if we are to read *King Lear*. Pseudo-statements to which we attach no belief and statements proper, such as science provides, cannot conflict. It is only when we introduce inappropriate kinds of believing into poetry that danger arises. To do so is from this point of view a profanation of poetry.

Yet an important branch of criticism which has attracted the best talents from prehistoric times until to-day consists of the endeavour to persuade men that the functions of science and poetry are identical, or that the one is a "higher form" of the other, or that they conflict and we must choose between them.

The root of this persistent endeavour has still to be mentioned; it is the same as that from which the Magical View of the world arose. If we give to a pseudo-statement the kind of unqualified acceptance which belongs by right only to certified scientific statements— and those judgments of the routine of perception and action from which science derives—if we can contrive to do this, the impulses and attitudes with which we respond to it gain a notable stability and vigour. Briefly, if we can contrive to believe poetry, then the world *seems*, while we do so, to be transfigured. It used to be comparatively easy to do this, and the habit has become well established. With the extension of science and the neutralization of nature it has become difficult as well as dangerous. Yet it is still alluring; it has many analogies with drug-taking. Hence the endeavours of the critics referred to. Various subterfuges have been devised along the lines of regarding Poetic Truth as figurative, symbolic; or as more immediate, as a truth of intuition transcending common knowledge; or as a higher form of the same truth that science yields. Such attempts to use poetry as a denial or as a corrective of science are very common. One point can be made against them all: they are never worked out in detail. There is no equivalent of Mill's *Logic* expounding any of them. The language in which they are framed is usually a blend of obsolete psychology and emotive exclamations.

The long-established and much-encouraged habit of giving to emotive utterances—whether pseudo-statements simple, or looser and larger wholes taken as saying something figuratively—the kind of assent which we give to unescapable facts, has for most people debilitated a wide range of their responses. A few scientists, caught young and brought up in the laboratory, are free from it; but then, as a rule, they pay no *serious* attention to poetry. For most men the recognition of the neutrality of nature brings about—through this habit —a divorce from poetry. They are so used to having their responses propped up by beliefs, however vague, that when these shadowy supports are removed they are no longer able to respond. Their attitudes to so many things have been forced in the past, over-encouraged. And when the world-picture ceases to assist there is a collapse. Over whole tracts of natural emotional response we are today like a bed of dahlias whose sticks

have been removed. And this effect of the neutraliza-
tion of nature is perhaps only in its beginnings. How-
ever, human nature has a prodigious resilience. Love
poetry seems able to out-play psychoanalysis.

A sense of desolation, of uncertainty, of futility, of
the groundlessness of aspirations, of the vanity of en-
deavour, and a thirst for a life-giving water which
seems suddenly to have failed, are the signs in con-
sciousness of this necessary reorganization of our lives.[3]
Our attitudes and impulses are being compelled to be-
come self-supporting; they are being driven back upon
their biological justification, made once again sufficient
to themselves. And the only impulses which seem strong
enough to continue unflagging are commonly so crude
that, to more finely developed individuals, they hardly
seem worth having. Such people cannot live by warmth,

---

3. My debt to *The Waste Land* here will be evident. The origi-
nal footnote seems to have puzzled Mr. Eliot and some other readers.
Well it might! In saying, though, that he "had effected a complete
severance between his poetry and all beliefs" I was referring not to
the poet's own history, but to the technical detachment of the poetry.
And the way in which he then seemed to me to have "realized what
might otherwise have remained a speculative possibility" was by find-
ing a new order through the contemplation and exhibition of dis-
order.
    "Yes! Very funny this terrible thing is. A man that is born falls
into a dream like a man who falls into the sea. If he tries to climb
out into the air as inexperienced people endeavour to do, he drowns
—*nicht wahr?* . . . No! I tell you! The way is to the destructive ele-
ment submit yourself, and with the exertions of your hands and feet
in the water make the deep, deep sea keep you up. So if you ask me
how to be? In the destructive element immerse . . . that was the
way." *Lord Jim*, p. 216. Mr. Eliot's later verse has sometimes shown
still less "dread of the unknown depths." That, at least, seems in part
to explain to me why *Ash Wednesday* is better poetry than even the
best sections of *The Waste Land*.

food, fighting, drink and sex alone. Those who are least affected by the change are those who are emotionally least removed from the animals. As we shall see at the close of this essay, even a considerable poet may attempt to find relief by a reversion to primitive mentality.

It is important to diagnose the disease correctly and to put the blame in the right quarter. Usually it is some alleged "materialism" of science which is denounced. This mistake is due partly to clumsy thinking, but chiefly to relics of the Magical View. For even if the Universe were "spiritual" all through (whatever that assertion might mean; all such assertions are probably nonsense), that would not make it any more accordant to human attitudes. It is not what the universe is made of but how it works, the law it follows, which makes verifiable knowledge of it incapable of spurring on our emotional responses, and further, the nature of knowledge itself makes it inadequate. The contact with things which we therein establish is too sketchy and indirect to help us. We are beginning to know too much about the bond which unites the mind to its object in knowledge [4] for that old dream of a perfect knowledge which would guarantee perfect life to retain its sanction. What was thought to be pure knowledge we see now to have been shot through with hope and desire, with fear and wonder; and these intrusive

4. Verifiable scientific knowledge, of course. Shift the sense of "knowledge" to include hope and desire and fear as well as reference, and what I am saying would no longer be true. But then the relevant sense of "true" would have changed too. Its sanction would no longer be verifiability.

elements indeed gave it all its power to support our lives. In knowledge, in the "How?" of events, we can find hints by which to take advantage of circumstances in our favour and avoid mischances. But we cannot get from it a *raison d'être* or a justification of more than a relatively lowly kind of life.

The justification, or the reverse, of any attitude lies, not in the object, but in itself, in its serviceableness to the whole personality. Upon its place in the whole system of attitudes, which is the personality, all its worth depends. This is as true for the subtle, finely compounded attitudes of the civilized individual as for the simpler attitudes of the child.

In brief, the imaginative life is its own justification; and this fact must be faced, although sometimes—by a lover, for example—it may be very difficult to accept. When it is faced, it is apparent that all the attitudes to other human beings and to the world in all its aspects, which have been serviceable to humanity, remain as they were, as valuable as ever. Hesitation felt in admitting this is a measure of the strength of the evil habit I have been describing. But many of these attitudes, valuable as ever, are, now that they are being set free, more difficult to maintain, because we still hunger after a basis in belief.

VII. SOME MODERN POETS

> . . . spitting from the mouth the withered
> apple-seed.
>
> T. S. ELIOT, *Ash Wednesday*

IT IS TIME to turn to those poets through study of
whose work these reflections arose. Hardy is for every
reason the poet with whom it is most natural to begin.
Not only did his work span the whole period in which
what I have called the neutralization of nature was fi-
nally effected, but it definitely reflected that change
throughout. Short essays in verse are fairly frequent
among his *Collected Poems*, essays almost always deal-
ing with this very topic; but these, however suggestive,
are not the ground for singling him out as the poet who
has most fully and courageously accepted the contem-
porary background; nor are the poems which are most
definitely *about* the neutrality of nature the ground for
the assertion. There is an opportunity for a misunder-
standing at this point. The ground is the tone, the
handling and the rhythm of poems which treat other
subjects, for example, "The Self Unseeing," "The

Voice," "A Broken Appointment," and pre-eminently "After a Journey." A poem does not necessarily accept a situation because it gives it explicit recognition, but only through the precise mutation of the attitudes of which it is composed. Mr. Middleton Murry, against some of whose positions parts of this essay may be suspected by the reader to be aimed, has best pointed out, in his *Aspects of Literature*, how peculiarly "adequate to what we know and have suffered" Hardy's poetry is. "His reaction to an episode has behind it and within it a reaction to the universe." This is not as I should put it were I making a statement; but read as a pseudo-statement, emotively, it is excellent; it makes us remember how we felt. Actually, it describes just what Hardy, at his best, does not do. He makes no reaction to the universe as an object for contemplation, recognizing it as something to which no reaction is more relevant than another. Mr. Murry is again well inspired, this time both emotively and scientifically, when he says: "Mr. Hardy stands high above all other modern poets by the deliberate purity of his responsiveness. The contagion of the world's slow stain has not touched him; from the first he held aloof from the general conspiracy to forget in which not only those who are professional optimists take a part." These extracts (from a writer more agonizingly aware than others that some strange change has befallen man in this generation, though his diagnosis is, I believe, mistaken) indicate very well Hardy's place and rank in English poetry. He is the poet who has most steadily refused to be comforted in an age in which the temptation to seek comfort has been greatest. The comfort of forgetfulness, the comfort of beliefs, he has put both these away. Hence his singular preoccupation with death; because it is in the contemplation of death that the necessity for human attitudes to become self-supporting, in the face of an indifferent universe, is felt most poignantly. Only the greatest tragic poets have achieved an equally self-reliant and immitigable acceptance.

From Hardy to Mr. De la Mare many seem a large transition, though readers of Mr. De la Mare's later work will agree that there are interesting resemblances —in "Who's That" and in other poems in *The Veil* where Mr. De la Mare is notably less himself than when writing at his best. In his poetry, in "The Pigs and the Charcoal Burner," in "John Mouldy," no intimation of the contemporary situation sounds. He is writing of, and from, a world which knows nothing of these difficulties, a world of pure phantasy for which the distinction between knowledge and feeling has not yet dawned. When in other poems, more reflective, in "The Tryst," for example, Mr. De la Mare does seem to be directly facing the indifference of the universe towards "poor mortal longingness," a curious thing happens. His utterance, in spite of his words, becomes not at all a recognition of this indifference, but voices instead an impulse to turn away, to forget it, to seek shelter in the warmth of his own familiar thickets of dream, not to stay out in the wind. His rhythm, that indescribable personal note which clings to all his best poetry, is a lulling rhythm, an anodyne, an opiate, it gives sleep and visions, phantasmagoria; but it does not give *vision*, it does not awaken. Even when he most appears to be contemplating the fate of the modern, "whom the words of the wise have made dumb," the drift of his verse is still "seeking after that sweet golden clime" where the mental traveller's journey *begins*.

There is one exception to this charge (for in a sense it is an adverse criticism, though not one to be pressed except against a great poet), there is one poem in which there is no such reluctance to bear the blast—"The Mad Prince's Song" in *Peacock Pie*. But here the spirit of the poem, the impulse which gives it life, comes from a poet who more than most refused to take shelter; "The Mad Prince's Song" derives from *Hamlet*.

Mr. Yeats and D. H. Lawrence present two further ways of dodging those difficulties which come from being born into this generation rather than into some earlier age. Mr. De la Mare takes shelter in the dream-world of the child, Mr. Yeats retired, for a season, into black velvet curtains and the visions of the Hermetist, and Lawrence made a magnificent attempt to reconstruct in himself the mentality of the Bushman. There are other modes to escape open to the poet. Mr. Blunden, to name one other poet only, goes into the country, but few people follow him there in his spirit, whereas Mr. Yeats and Lawrence, whether they are widely read or not, do represent tendencies among the defeated which are only too easily observable.

Mr. Yeats' work from the beginning was a repudia-

tion of the most active contemporary interests. But at
first the poet of "The Wanderings of Usheen," "The
Stolen Child" and "Innisfree" turned away from con-
temporary civilization in favour of a world which he
knew perfectly, the world of folk-lore as it is accepted,
neither with belief nor disbelief, by the peasant. Folk-
lore and the Irish landscape, its winds, woods, waters,
islets and seagulls, and for a while an unusually simple
and direct kind of love poetry in which he became more
than a minor poet, these were his refuge. Later, after
a drawn battle with the drama, he made a more violent
repudiation, not merely of current civilization but of
life itself, a favour of a supernatural world. But the
world of the "eternal moods," of supernal essences and
immortal beings was not, like the Irish peasant stories
and the Irish landscape, part of his natural and familiar
experience. He turned to a world of symbolic phantas-
magoria about which he was desperately uncertain. The
uncertainty came in part from the adoption, as a tech-
nique of inspiration, of the use of trance, of dissociated
phases of consciousness. The revelations given in these
dissociated states are insufficiently connected with nor-
mal experience. This, in part, explains the weakness of
Mr. Yeats' transcendental poetry. A deliberate reversal
of the natural relations of thought and feeling may be
the rest of the explanation. Mr. Yeats took certain feel-
ings—feelings of conviction attaching to certain visions
—as evidence for the thoughts which he supposed his
visions to symbolize. To Mr. Yeats the value of "The
Phases of the Moon" lay not in any attitudes which it

arouses or embodies but in the doctrine which for an initiate it promulgates.

The resort to trance and the effort to discover a new world-picture to replace that given by science are two most significant points for our purpose in Mr. Yeats' work.[1] A third might be the singularly bitter contempt for the generality of mankind which occasionally appears.

The doctrinal problem arises again, but in a clearer form with Lawrence. But here we have the advantage of an elaborate prose exposition, *Fantasia of the Unconscious,* of the positions which so many of the poems advocate. It is not unfair to put the matter in this way, since there is little doubt possible that the bulk of Lawrence's published verse is prose, scientific prose too, jottings, in fact, from a psychologist's notebook, with a commentary interspersed. Due allowance being made for the extreme psychological interest of these observations, there remains the task of explaining how the poet who wrote the "Ballad of Another Ophelia" and "Aware," some pages of *Birds, Beasts and Flowers,* and *The White Peacock,* should have wandered, through his own zeal misdirected, so far from the paths which once appeared to be his alone to open.

Lawrence's revolt against civilization seems to have been originally spontaneous, an emotional revulsion free from *ad hoc* beliefs. It sprang directly from experience.

1. Who could have foreseen before *The Tower* Mr. Yeats' development into the greatest poet of our age or the miracles in *Songs for Music Perhaps?*

He came to abhor all the attitudes men adopt, not through the direct prompting of their instincts, but because of the supposed nature of the objects to which they are directed. The conventions, the idealizations, which come between man and man and between man and woman, which often queer the pitch for the natural responses, seemed to him the source of all evil. Part of his revolt was certainly justified. These idealizations—representative examples are the dogma of the equality of man and the doctrine that Love is primarily sympathy—are beliefs illicitly interpolated in order to support and strengthen attitudes in the manner discussed at length above. And Lawrence's original rejection of a morality not self-supporting but based upon beliefs makes his work an admirable illustration of my main thesis. But two simple and avoidable mistakes deprived his revolt of the greater part of its value. He overlooked the fact that such beliefs commonly arise because the attitudes they support are already existent. He assumed that a bad basis for an attitude meant a bad attitude. In general, it does mean a forced attitude, but that is another matter. Secondly, he tried to cure the disease by introducing other beliefs of his own manufacture in place of the conventional beliefs and in support of very different attitudes.

The genesis of these beliefs is extremely interesting as an illustration of primitive mentality. Since the attitudes on which he fell back are those of a very early stage of human development, it is not surprising that the means by which he supported them should be of

the same era, or that of the world-picture which he
worked out should be similar to that described in *The
Golden Bough*. The mental process at work is sche-
matically as follows: First, undergo an intense emo-
tion, located with unusual definiteness in the body,
which can be described as "a feeling *as though* the
solar plexus were connected by a current of dark pas-
sional energy with another person." Those whose emo-
tions tend to be localized will be familiar with such
feelings. The second step is to say, "I must trust my
feelings." The third is to call the feeling an intuition.
The last is to say, "*I know* that my solar plexus is, etc."
By this means we arrive at indubitable knowledge that
the sun's energy is recruited from the life on the earth
and that the astronomers are wrong in what they say
about the moon, and so on.

The illicit steps in the argument are not quite so
evident as they appear to be in this analysis. To dis-
tinguish an intuition *of* an emotion from an intuition
by it is not always easy, nor is a description of an emo-
tion always in practice distinguishable from an emo-
tion. Certainly we must trust our feelings—in the sense
of acting upon them. We have nothing else to trust.
And to confuse this trusting with believing an emo-
tive description of them is a mistake which all tradi-
tional codes of morality encourage us to commit.

The significance of such similar disasters in the work
of poets so unlike and yet so greatly gifted as Mr.
Yeats and Lawrence is noteworthy. For each, the tradi-
tional scaffolding of conventional beliefs proved unsat-

isfying, unworkable as a basis for their attitudes. Each sought, in very different directions it is true, a new set of beliefs as a remedy. For neither did the world-picture of science seem a possible substitute. And neither seems to have envisaged the possibility of a poetry which is independent of all such supporting beliefs,[2] probably because, however much they differ, both are very serious poets. A great deal of poetry can, of course, be written for which total independence of all beliefs is an easy matter. But it is never poetry of the more important kind, because the temptation to introduce beliefs is a sign and measure of the importance of the attitudes involved. At present it is not primarily religious beliefs, in stricter and narrower senses of the word, which are most likely to be concerned. Emphases alter surprisingly. University societies founded in 1910, for example, to discuss religion, were discussing sex when this was first written in 1926, as they are discussing political ideologies today (1935).

Yet the necessity for independence is increasing. This is not to say that traditional poetry, into which beliefs readily enter, is becoming obsolete; it is merely becoming more and more difficult to approach without confusion; it demands a greater imaginative effort, a greater purity in the reader.

We must distinguish here, however. There are many feelings and attitudes which, though in the past supported by beliefs now untenable, can survive their re-

2. Mr. Yeats' later triumphs, especially the Cracked Mary (or Crazy Jane) songs, seem to me to be such a poetry.

moval because they have other, more natural, supports and spring directly from the necessities of existence. To the extent to which they have been undistorted by the beliefs which have gathered round them they will remain as before. But there are other attitudes which are very largely the product of belief and have no other support. These will lapse if the changes here forecasted continue. With their disappearance some forms of poetry—much minor devotional verse, for example—will become obsolete. And with the unravelling of the intellect *versus* emotion entanglement, there will be cases where even literature to which immense value has been assigned—the speculative portions of the work of Dostoevsky may be instanced—will lose much of its interest, except for the history of the mind. It was because he belonged to his age that Dostoevsky had to wrestle so terribly in these toils. A poet today, whose integrity is equal to that of the greater poets of the past, is inevitably plagued by the problem of thought and feeling [3] as poets have never been plagued before.

A pioneer in modern research upon the origins of culture was asked recently whether his work had any bearing upon religion. He replied that it had, but that at present he was engaged merely in "getting the guns into position." The same answer might be given with regard to the probable consequences of recent progress

3. Of verifiability and faith, I would say, if it were clear that the faith was never in anything that could possibly be verified or, conversely, that the verification was of a kind that had no relevance to the faith.

in psychology, not only for religion but for the whole fabric of our traditional beliefs about ourselves. In many quarters there is a tendency to suppose that the series of attacks upon received ideas which began, shall we say, with Galileo and rose to a climax with Darwinism, has overreached itself with Einstein and Eddington, and that the battle is now due to die down. This view seems to be too optimistic. The most dangerous of the sciences is only now beginning to come into action. I am thinking not so much of psychoanalysis or of behaviourism as of the whole subject which includes them.

The Hindenburg Line to which the defence of our traditions retired as the result of the onslaughts of the last century may still be officially held (in the schools, for example), but it is really abandoned as worth neither defence nor attack. The struggle is elsewhere, and it is no longer over matters suited to intellectual debate. "What to believe?"—which could be argued—has given place to "With what different kinds of believings must we order the different ranks of our myths [4]?" and that is decided not by arguing but in living. The lowest rank and the least challengeable or optional or dispensable— that routine of perception which guards the safety of our every bodily step, that order of expectations or of assumptions in virtue of which we catch or miss our trains—has unequalled authority over its own members. It lends this authority to the sciences which derive from

4. Not necessarily a derogatory word; see *Coleridge on Imagination*, Chapter VII.

it—though not, of course, to their optional, speculative aspects. And these sciences progressively invade every province of our thought. They meet nothing with equal authority, or that can resist them, which does not take its power from the same source in verifiable happenings.

In so far as any question comes within their peculiar authority they decide it; and a peculiar believing or acceptance there belongs. Challenge from myths of other ranks is suicidal. They challenge by mistake as to their own rank (which would, if they kept it, be higher, as concerned with more inclusive interests) and thus degrade the kinds of believing they embody. The danger is that science, as it has more to tell us about ourselves, may more and more invite this mistake and so provoke other myths to defy it and then force them to surrender. But their work is not that of science; as they do not give us what science gives, so science cannot give us what they give.

If a conflict which should never have arisen extends much further, a moral chaos such as man has never experienced may be expected. Our protection, as Matthew Arnold, in my epigraph, insisted, is in poetry. It is capable of saving us, or since some have found a scandal in this word, of preserving us or rescuing us from confusion and frustration. The poetic function is the source, and the tradition of poetry is the guardian, of the suprascientific myths. "The poetry of a people takes its life from the people's speech and in turn gives life to it; and represents its highest point of consciousness, its greatest power and its most delicate sensibility." So wrote the best poet of my generation recently.[5] That we should consider further what this power is, what it has given us, and what threatens it, is all my argument.

5. T. S. Eliot, *The Use of Poetry*, p. 15.

APPENDIX

Two CHIEF WORDS seem likely occasions of misunderstanding in the above; and they have in fact misled some readers. One is *Nature*, the other is *Belief*.

Nature is evidently as variable a word as can be used. Its senses range from the mere inclusive THAT, in which we live and of which we are a part, to whatever would correspond to the most detailed and interconnected account we could attain of this. Or we omit ourselves (and other minds) and make Nature *either* what influences us (in which case we should not forget our metabolism), *or* an object we apprehend (in which case there are as many Natures as there are types of apprehension we care to distinguish). And what is "natural" to one culture is strange and artificial to another. (See *Mencius on the Mind*, Chapter III). More deceptively, the view here being inseparable from the eye, and this being a matter of habitual speculation, we may talk, as we think, the same language and yet put very different things into Nature; and what we then find will not be unconnected with what we have put in.

I have attempted some further discussion of these questions in Chapters VI and VII of *Coleridge on Imagination*.

Belief. Two "beliefs" may differ from one another: (1) in their objects, (2) in their statements or expressions, (3) in their modes, (4) in their grounds, (5) in their occasions, (6) in their connections with other "beliefs," (7) in their links with possible action, (8) and in other ways. Our chief evidence usually for the beliefs of other people (and often for our own) must be some statement or other expression. But very different beliefs may fittingly receive the same expression. Most words used in stating any speculative opinion are as ambiguous as "belief"; and yet by such words belief-objects must be distinguished.

But in the case of "belief" there is an additional difficulty. Neither it nor its partial synonyms suggest the great variety of the attitudes (3) that are commonly covered (and confused) by the term. They are often treated as though they were mere variations in degree. Of what? Of belief, it would be said. But this is no better than the parallel trick of treating all varieties of love as a mere more or less only further differentiated by their objects. Such crude over-simplifications distort the structure of the mind and, although favourite suasive devices with some well-intentioned preachers, are disastrous.

There is an ample field here awaiting a type of dispassionate inquiry which it has seldom received. A world threatened with ever more and more leisure should not be too impatient of important and explorable subtleties.

Meanwhile, as with "Nature," misunderstandings should neither provoke nor surprise. I should not be much less at my reader's mercy if I were to add notes doubling the length of this little book. On so vast a matter, even the largest book could contain no more than a sketch of how things have seemed to be sometimes to the writer.

Commentary

NOTES ON THE TEXT (1970)

Page 16, line 19 †

Analogous reconceptions have, since 1926, made these
examples tame. A list of current transformations of
possibility would, if I inserted it here, be out of date
in far less than forty years. It is a major problem, not
for statesmen and their advisers only, that the fron-
tiers of possibility are now receding with such accelera-
tion. No one should confidently set limits to what man
may soon be able to do: *for good*, let us bear in mind,
as much as for evil.

Page 17, line 13

Perhaps, as often with instances of emphasis, the italics
here witness chiefly to disturbance of reflection. Both
the average educated man and *more conscious* invite
analysis which might well lead to head-shaking over
both concepts.

---

† Page and line references locate the annotated word or phrase in
the text.

Page 18, line 26

understanding. Comprehending would seem to me now a better word here, partly because *understanding* may suggest a rather limited sort of theoretical approach, partly because of the analysis of comprehending offered in my *Speculative Instruments*, Essay II.

Page 19, line 1

practical consequences. Someday—maybe soon—someone will be able to give us an evidence-supported account of (a) how changes of fashion in psychology have influenced fashions in conduct; (b) how changes in physical theory have influenced attitudes to Nature. We could then make some comparisons. As yet we can only conjecture in both fields. No doubt psychoanalysis (*not*, see below, what I was thinking of here) did have deep effects in people's behavior and on their attitudes to it. Perhaps behaviorism, on a far smaller scale, led to some lowering of responsibility in self-criticism. Perhaps the new models for the mind are re-moralizing the design and evaluation of conduct. The original paragraph fails to recognize that the "practical consequences" it alludes to could be, as with some forms of compulsion and some types of programming, too frightening to be easily imagined.

Page 21, line 24

show. This looks a more reasonable assumption than it turns out to be. The word *show* is playing one of its most deceiving tricks (see *How to Read a Page*, pp. 138–141) and, in spite of the seeming modesty of "to some extent," *it* in "what it is" eludes ordinary attempts to identify what is being spoken of.

Page 23, line 28

the sound of the words. Immense advances in phonology during these forty years reinforce this point. The connexities between "parts" of a poem stressed in "Reorientation" are in a large measure meditated through phonological and articulatory relationships.

Page 25, line 22

governor. The prodigious development of studies of control (in cybernetics and systems engineering) since 1926 can now point up this parallel.

Page 26, line 10

an arrangement . . . . It seems a pity that such mobiles are not more available as educational toys.

Page 27, line 24

This development. But, of course, his acquisition of speech is the epochal change—to be followed in the favoured by reading-writing, that decisive acquisition of a notation, success in which can remake him or failure maim him. Compare on what notations can do for us my *Design for Escape* (1968) pages 18 and 121. For a more general discussion of notations see "Meanings Anew" in my *So Much Nearer: Essays Towards a*

World English, New York, Harcourt, Brace & World, Inc., 1968, pages 132–139.

Page 31, line 9

Shakespeare's songs. As a corrective to what may be excessive here see my comments on Housman's misleading remarks in his *The Name and Nature of Poetry*, Chapter IX, "The Bridle of Pegasus"; *Coleridge on Imagination*, pp. 200–201, 205, 209–11.

Page 33, line 25

if they actually . . . . I would now omit the parenthetic remarks. The precise condition, motives, etc., etc. animating a composer are, I think, beside the point. We do not know enough to hazard such conjectures. It is from how the words work that we may try to guess how they may have been put together; not the other way round.

Page 37, line 2

Biologists . . . . Fuller discussion of this crucial point will be found in the opening essay "From Criticism to Creation" of my *So Much Nearer: Essays Toward a World English*, New York, Harcourt, Brace & World, Inc., 1968.

Page 38, line 5

lifelessness. We should, however, recall and weigh with care what Socrates had to say: "See this: death is either nothingness, complete unconsciousness; or it's a change,

a migration of the soul to some other place. If it is un-
consciousness, like a sleep in which you don't even
dream, death is a very great gain. For if you take a
night which you slept through without a dream and
ask how many other days and nights of your life were
better than that, I believe even the Great King of
Persia himself would find that they were few. If that
is what death is like, I say it is a gain. All time becomes
no more than one night." *Apology*. From my *Why So,
Socrates? A Dramatic Version*, Cambridge, England,
Cambridge University Press, 1964.

Page 40, line 1

winning victories. I did not then recall Plato: "Tem-
perance, I take it, is a sort of beautiful order, a control,
as men say, over certain desires and pleasures. So a man
is said to be master of himself, a strange way of talking,
because, if he is master of himself, he is equally the slave
of himself, for it is one and the same person who is
being talked of." *Republic*, 431. From my version in
simple English, Cambridge, England, Cambridge Uni-
versity Press, 1967.

Page 44, line 1

idle to ask him. "Socrates: After the politicians I went
to the poets. I took lines from their own writings and
asked them what they meant, hoping to learn some-
thing from them. Do you know: the truth is, almost
anyone there could have talked better than they did—
even about the very poems they had written them-

selves." "Apology," from my *Why So, Socrates? A Dramatic Version*, Cambridge, England, Cambridge University Press, 1964.

Page 51, line 9

the last seventy. A 1935 dating.

Page 53, line 32

footnote. I would now rather refer to my *How to Read a Page* and to "Toward a Theory of Comprehending" in my *Speculative Instruments* (Harcourt, Brace & World, Inc., 1967). See also Appendix B. "How Does a Poem Know When It Is Finished?"

Page 55, line 30

footnote. For a fuller discussion of this see *Interpretation in Teaching* (1938), Chapter 21, "Logical Machinery and Empty Words," pp. 353–54.

Page 57, line 14

linguistic psychology. Psychology, to carry out such a duty, will have to absorb much of what is currently labelled linguistics. In return, linguistics, being thus absorbed, will have to become radically more empirical and humble than has of late been its wont.

Page 57, line 21

as sensory stimuli and as (in the widest sense) symbols. As phonological and as semantic agents? See "Meanings

Anew" in *So Much Nearer* (Harcourt, Brace & World,
Inc., 1968). As has been remarked above, advances in
phonology through the last forty years have much
strengthened these reasons. But these gains have made
the phrases "sensory stimuli" and "sensory side" more
likely than before to be misleading. It is the connexi-
ties among the phonologic and articulatory components
which enable them to play, in conjunction with the
"symbolic," semantic oppositions, such a key role. The
three systems of requirements and exclusions: phono-
logic, syntactic and semantic work together very in-
timately in most modes of poetic utterance.

Page 58, line 7

pseudo-statement. Misrepresentations of the position
taken both here and in *Principles* are still frequent:
"The view that poetry and literature in general, what-
ever they purport to refer to, are in fact referring solely
to the author's feelings first began to gain general ac-
ceptance in English literary circles with the publication
of I. A. Richards' *Principles of Literary Criticism* in
1925. . . . Richards' opponents have since pointed out
that unfortunately the 'emotive' power of a poetic state-
ment depends precisely on our interpretating it as an
objective reference to something *other* than emotion it-
self" (Owen Barfield, "The Riddle of the Sphinx,"
Arena, P.E.N., April 1964, p. 121). I have not been
writing about miscomprehension these fifty years to be
surprised now by such extravagations. Nor will I be the
only one to have become accustomed to being accused

of the views he was attacking or to having pointed out to him just what he has himself been pointing out.

Page 60, line 6

malpractice. "We have learned to distinguish these days between concepts which are verifiable and those by nature unverifiable—and which therefore can't be argued about: so really we need two words for 'belief' and two for 'truth,' since we don't mean the same things by 'belief' and 'truth' in both cases." (*The Fox in the Attic* by Richard Hughes, Chapter 21, p. 77, Harper & Row, 1961) Mr. Hughes gives Mary these thoughts as of 1923. My present view would be that we really use more than two meanings with such words. This masterly novel may remind us that it was some of the poetries that gave Hitler his power as it was some of the sciences that made the slaughter possible.

Page 61, line 10

equally fine organization. I do not think that any who have been noting the recrudescence and the return of violence and ruthlessness in so many parts of what was called "the civilised world" will consider these dreary surmises to have been exaggeration.

REORIENTATION

MUCH IN MY ACCOUNT OF "The Poetic Experience" is
a simplification of doctrines more elaborately expounded
in *Principles of Literary Criticism*. Some of these have
since seemed to me not so much false as undeveloped
and likely to be wrongly taken. In what follows I try
to add some of the misleading parts of the picture and
with them to redirect the whole design. What should
then appear could be, it may be hoped, somewhat more
useful to poets than the earlier sketches.

In chief, the connexities *within* any experience that
is likely to be called "poetic" in any relevant sense were
not brought out enough; nor were the multiplicities and
intricacies of its dependencies upon other experience.
The author does, it is true, mention ʳinnumerable in-
terconnectionsʳ between his ˢʷintellectualˢʷ and his
ˢʷactive or emotionalˢʷ streams and speak of their sep-
aration as no more than ʳan expositor's artificeʳ.† But
the whole layout of the account fights against a sufficient
recognition of these mutual influences; and it is this I
must now try to redress.

† See Note on Specialized Quotation Marks below.

Take first what we may rather too easily call
^{di}parts^{di} of the poem without more than dimly and
distantly realizing what a variety of choices we may
be offering our interlocutor as to what we are talking
of. Its lines are parts; so are its assumptions, it implica-
tions, its suggestions, its echoes, its words, its letters, its
commas . . . but in what different ways! † And often,
relations between parts are themselves parts: the length
of a line may come to it from other lines (in a sense
quite unlike anything to be settled by some measure-
ment), a foot takes its form from other feet, actual or
possible; an assonance works by not being a full rhyme.
. . . As a shift of mood requires the former mood, so
a word may succeed by *not* being the expected word.
Or by being, surprisingly, just *that*. Such gambits and
stratagems are omnipresent and inexhaustibly various
in all speech. A wide and often convenient definition
of the ^{sw}poetic^{sw} use of language makes it simply dis-
course in which such features heighten the efficiency
of the utterance.

To consider how the composing mind, and the re-
composing mind of the recipient, manage such devices
will be a means of bringing home the connexities I note
as under-stressed in *Science and Poetry*. In the use (and
in the recipient's interpretation)—witting, unwitting or
betwixt and between—of an alliteration, say, or an as-

† See *Parts & Wholes: the Hayden Colloquium on Scientific
Method and Concept*, edited by Daniel Lerner, New York, The Free
Press, 1963. The contribution of Roman Jakobson is particularly
relevant. I am including my own talk, which followed his, as sup-
plying illustration of the points this Reorientation is helping to make.

sonance a great deal more recognition of structure must enter than we commonly suppose. The structures in question will commonly be cyclic: eddyings, to borrow from Coleridge,[†] eddyings often of eddies of eddies— each sub-component having the reciprocal, interdependent features of ^{nb}feed-forward^{nb} and ^{nb}feed-back^{nb}: i.e., what has happened has set the cycle *for* (fed forward) a consequent. Occurrence, accordant or otherwise at the set point, is reported (fed back) to the larger system sustaining the sub-cycle so that corrective action, if need be, may be taken.

Perhaps the most pertinent illustration of a feed-forward feed-back cycle is the drawing of a free-hand circle.[‡] First comes the feed-forward directive as to the size of the circle. It cannot be begun without that. Then with every inch your chalk travels there is feed-back reporting to your nerve-muscle-tendon-joint executives as to violations of the feed-forward directives and an issuing of new feed-forward as to corrective action if needed. Conceive now that, as serving the free but controlled sweep of your arm, all the contributors —your eye on the alert for aberrations; your nerves as balancing the opposing pulls of the muscles that roll shoulder, elbow, wrist, thumb and finger joints—are all organized in cooperative circuits. Probably we should think of even the smaller sub-components of these circuits as being also cyclic systems held stable through

[†] "Dejection," line 136, "Their life the eddying of her living soul."
[‡] See *English Through Pictures*, Book 2. New York, Pocket Books, p. 229.

their dependence upon the wider systems within what they serve.

What is most plainly evident about the over-all arrangement is the immense amount of *substitution* † it permits. Alternative means are richly available. You can, for example, correct your curve by adjustment at shoulder, elbow or wrist or in varying degrees at all three. If for any reason a step cannot be taken in one way, it can in another. Obviously, this is of the greatest biologic importance. What has, however, to be imagined (as far as may be) is *how* these alternates get selected and alerted and how their precedences, mergers, etc. are ordered. Some sort of communication-system, maybe a variety of them, between sub-systems within, across and up and down the multiplicities of hierarchies of control seems to be required. All this, of course, is yet (1970) highly conjectural; but such has been the utterly unexpected rate of advance in these matters in recent years and such the promise of contemporary neurological model designs that new, and perhaps liberating, light on human potential may be looked for quite soon.

No doubt it is premature and perhaps absurd to call the mind-brain a parallel calculator; but at least the analogies are such that we can now imagine much more resourcefully than before *how* it contrives to do what it does and also how truly preternatural, in the sense of beyond our previous notions of the natural, these doings are.

---

† The point is how much room for correction is provided, as Von Neumann pointed out, when many independent parallel circuits co-operate simultaneously.

Among these preternaturals, some of the poetries offer the most reflexive, self-involved examples. Indeed, these are self-editing, sometimes to a degree matched only at the opposite end of the mental spectrum: in mathematics. The modes of self-reference and self-examination are, however, fully as diverse. Mathematics explores itself by mathematical means, poetries by poetic. This self-searching shows itself whenever in composing, or in choice between interpretations, we note how we are guided by the extent to which change in one component entails change in others, whenever we 'see' that if x varies, p,g . . . must vary too. The process of composition is indeed a weighing of these entailments, a balancing imposed by the rivalling possibilities of the alternates. I suggest that, as with our circle-drawing, we should include alternates of which we do not ordinarily or normally admit we are in the least cognizant.

We are not cognizant of them, but the composing, the growth of the poem, is. Something then in *us* takes account of the innumerable entailments: cooperations and repudiations, in an unhesitating and secure fashion.

What 'we' or 'us' in such sentences can be talking about is no easy matter to decide. It seems perhaps a likely suggestion that ^{w}we,^{w} in such instances, represents the system of relevant feed-forward, which at the moment is being confirmed by feed-back. Such a view would accord with the widely agreed fact that our ^{sw}we^{sw}s keep varying. The ^{sw}we^{sw} that is concerned with writing or interpreting a poem seems very closely bound up with what it is doing. By comparison ^{sw}we^{sw}

which uses its knowledge of the multiplication table seems little involved. Both, however, belong to the big ?WE? that no biographer can ever understand.

Adding, as I suggest we should, influential alternates ?we? do *not cognize* (though the poem does) may restore to the poem the mystery that most poetries seem justly to claim. The poem knows more than we do about itself, and part of its business is to make us feel so. Such a view of a poem rescues it, I hope, from that status as a "choice piece of experience" to which *S & P*, I fear, gave some countenance. (This was labelled and denounced, I hope damagingly, as the Vulgar Packaging View in "The Future of Poetry," (Appendix to *The Screens and Other Poems* and reprinted in *So Much Nearer*, Harcourt, Brace & World, Inc., 1968). The poem ceases to be a record and appears instead as a coming into itself of a being with a role of its own to play. It starts off as a problem: *what to be;* and ends by finding in itself, when successful, what it was seeking. It becomes self-entailed: in Coleridge's formula it "contains in itself the reason why it is so and not otherwise."

So much for the inner connexities which *S & P*, I think, missed. The further connexities, the linkages, selective and corrective, with what has been and is to be, these were—unless I am being unfair—as lightly passed over. The book was perhaps too busy hurrying up the retreat of religion to attend properly to its own business.

These further connexities, through which the poetries can pursue their task of exploring, re-assessing, and confirming values, can perhaps be suggested most compendiously by a reminder of what a good enough dictionary could display. Every word, it could show, is connected, directly or circuitously, in every one of its uses with uses of all other words. ˢʷUsesˢʷ here deserves careful reflection. A ˢʷuseˢʷ of the word here is some work it is being asked to do, some task it is required (in co-operation with other words) to help with. We may remind ourselves: (1) that these tasks we ask words to take part in are attempts to cope with situations; and (2) that these situations are complexes within which the utterer and the recipient are necessary and fundamental parts along with, and involved in, the thing to be done.

All this, which is perhaps as a rule ʹtaken for grantedʹ in thought about what language does for man, if spelled out and then pondered resourcefully, can become, I think, that justification of the poetries— as language well employed on creative tasks—which the author of *S & P* did not quite know where to look for, though he knew that it needs perennially to be sought.

Perhaps he was scared by some silly uses of ʷcreativeʷ and did not feel like venturing upon the others.

Say can'st thou make thyself?—Learn first that trade;—
Haply thou mayst know what thyself had made.†

Perhaps not even Coleridge knew just how to take that. And probably, few reflective readers will be at all constant in how they take it, though they may agree

† Coleridge, "Self Knowledge."

that among the things that language has to do, to help us in finding improved orders of being may be counted the chief. As Philosophy told Boethius in his prison: "Now do I know the cause of your sickness. You have forgotten what you are."

SPECIALIZED QUOTATION MARKS

We all recognise—more or less unsystematically— that quotation marks serve varied purposes:

1. Sometimes they show merely that we are quoting and where our quotation begins and ends.

2. Sometimes they imply that the word or words within them are in some way open to question and are only to be taken in some special sense with reference to some special definition.

3. Sometimes they suggest further that what is quoted is nonsense or that there is really no such thing as the thing they profess to name.

4. Sometimes they suggest that the words are improperly used. The quotation marks are equivalent to "the so-called."

5. Sometimes they indicate only that we are talking of the words as distinguished from their meanings. "Is" and "at" are shorter than "above." "Chien" means what "dog" means, and so on.

There are many other uses. This short list will suffice to show how heavily we overwork this too-serviceable writing device. Some of these uses accordingly are taken over by italics, but there again ambiguity easily arises. We italicize for emphasis (of several kinds) as well as to show that we are talking about words themselves or about some special use made of them. In speech, of course, many of these subtleties can be handled by intonation and pausing, though not with high uniformity or equally well by all speakers.

In most discussions of meanings, quotation marks will necessarily be given an inordinately heavy task to perform. This there is no avoiding. In all interpretation work we have to be able to hold up words and phrases for separate and special attention, and we have to do our best to indicate what our attitudes to them and to their meanings are. It is somewhat absurd, indeed, that writers have not long ago developed a notation system for this purpose which would distinguish the various duties these little commas hanging about our words are charged with.

I continue here with an experiment first tried in my *How to Read a Page* (Norton, 1942) in using a range of special symbols that take the place of the usual quotation marks. They will be small letters placed, as quotation marks are, about the words, the phrases and the sentences they single out. A key to this notation follows. It will be found in practice, I believe, that two glances at the key prepare the reader to recognize, without consulting it anew, what I suppose myself to be doing when I use the notation. It gives us a compact means of commenting on the handling of language—more comprehensible, less ambiguous and less distracting than the usual devices of parenthesis, qualification and discussion. I believe it will abridge both the optical and the intellectual labor of the reader.

KEY

ᵂ. . . . . .ᵂ   indicates that the word—merely as that word in general—is being talked about. The marks are equivalent to "the word." E.g., "ᵂtableᵂ may mean an article of furniture or a list."

ʳ. . . . . .ʳ   indicates that some special use of the word or phrase is being referred to. The marks are equivalent to "Please refer to the place in the passage we should have in mind here." E.g., "ʳNatureʳ for Whitehead is not Wordsworth's ʳNature.ʳ"

ˀ. . . . . .ˀ   indicates that our problem is What does this word say here? Not whether anything it seems to say is acceptable or not. The marks are equivalent to "Query: what meaning?" There is no derogatory implication. Most ˀimportantˀ words are, or should be, in this situation.

ᵎ. . . . . .ᵎ   indicates surprise or derision, a "Good Heavens! What-a-way-to-talk!" attitude. It may be read ᵎshriekᵎ if we have occasion to read it aloud.

^{nb}. . . . . .^{nb} indicates that how the word is understood is a turning point in the discussion, and usually that it may easily be read in more than one way or with an inadequate perception of its importance. The sign is short for *nota bene.*

^{sw}. . . . . .^{sw} indicates that the reader is invited to consider "Something that may be said *W*ith ^{sw}____.^{sw}" The marks are short for "Something said With." They are useful when we need to remind ourselves of the very different things that may be meant by the words we are using, and may well be read "Said warily."

^{i}. . . . . .^{i} indicates that other senses that the word may have in other occurrences may intervene. The marks are equivalent to "Intervention likely."
By extension

^{di}. . . . . .^{di} would mean "Danger! Watch out!" and

^{hi}. . . . . .^{hi} would mean "Helpful intervention."
In contrast, a word or phrase to be read as having no relevant relations to any other senses in other places, actual or possible, could be written

^{t}. . . . . .^{t} to mean "technical term" defined and fixed in this employment.

ⁿ. . . . . .ⁿ indicates that the word is the name that is being used and that we know what it names, though we may not think it a good name. The sign is equivalent to "the so-called ——."

Lastly why should we not use the mark =, equivalent to, to indicate that the words or phrases it links are to be taken as having the same ?meaning? for the purposes in hand? This escapes the unfortunate suggestion: that whatever the first is talking about 'really is' the second. The usual device is to write "(i.e., ——)," which too often carries the suggestion that somehow we have no need to ask ourselves what the second explanatory word or phrase is itself standing for here. An equally troublesome device is to add "(or ——)," which commonly offers us a dangerous, usually a crude, ambiguity. ʷOrʷ then may be presenting an alternative thing or just another *name* for the same thing.

HOW DOES A POEM KNOW
WHEN IT IS FINISHED? †

I CAN SET OUT FROM Edgar Allan Poe: "I have often thought how interesting a magazine paper might be written by an author who would—that is to say who could—detail, step by step, the processes by which one of his compositions attained its ultimate point of completion" (*The Philosophy of Composition*). "Who would—that is to say who could" how are we to read that? Should it suggest that anyone able to give such an account would be only too happy to oblige? Or, on the contrary, that few could bear to make such an exhibition of themselves? The continuation of the passage rather leans toward the latter.

However that may be, is not perhaps a change of attitude here due? The brands of psychology that have been most widely distributed of late have been some-

† Reprinted with the permission of The Macmillan Company from *Parts and Wholes: The Hayden Colloquium on Scientific Method and Concept*, edited by Daniel Lerner, © by Massachusetts Institute of Technology, 1963.

what discouraging to our taste for privacy. The general notion that not even our own minds are our own—together with the view that there aren't any minds at all anyhow—would rather invite us to indulge in whatever exposures may, if so, prove possible. Accordingly, toward the end of this paper, you will find some sort of account of how one of my own poems attained—I won't say "its ultimate point of completion" but only the point at which it committed itself to burial in the page—hoping, of course, for innumerable lives thereafter, countless resurrections in its readers' minds.

My guide in much that I will be saying and assuming is Coleridge's remark, in Chapter XIV of *Biographia Literaria:* "Nothing can permanently please, which does not contain in itself the reason why it is so, and not otherwise." Or, as Shelley rephrased it in the opening sentence of *A Defense of Poetry,* "each containing within itself the principle of its own integrity."

It may be useful to consider, to begin with, that many poems (maybe all, but with the word "all" we are in danger of giving up observation in favor of definition, so I will say only "many") set themselves initially a problem, the solving, or dismission, or dispersal of which would be—in happy instances is—the completion: the attainment of the wholeness we are concerned with. Relative to that end (as terminus and as purposive goal) prior phases—temporally or logically or psychologically or purposively prior in different instances—are parts.

Let us not try to be too specific, as yet, about these

problems that poems set themselves. We may expect them to be illimitably various in innumerable respects, in character, in scope, in importance and in definiteness. Some of these problems are relatively simple; some relatively complex.

The type specimen of a simple and definite problem is, I take it, the drawing of a circle, which, as an exemplar of unity, offers itself as one of the handiest of models. The enterprise of drawing a freehand circle defines itself to itself very early—within the first millimeter of circumference drawn—and, with that, the conduct of all the rest of it and the criteria of success are uniquely prescribed and so is the exact point of completion.

Perhaps the minimal problem a poem can set itself is the mere finding or creation (discovery or invention) of a situation which will permit its growth. I have mentioned the word "growth" so early because I find myself deeply persuaded that the analogies that help most here are biological, organic, more specifically, embryological.

The over-all problem of an embryo was long ago described by the Psalmist—in the course of giving his own answer:

> Thine eyes did see my substance
>   yet being unperfect;
> And in thy book were all my members written;
> Which day by day were fashioned:
> When as yet there was none of them.

"When as yet there was none of them," how do they know what to become next in the course of becoming what in the end they have to be? That is the problem of the embryo. The answer offered is an analogy with a formula, an inventory, a sequence of directions, directives, in a book. It isn't really a good answer, is it? For one reason, because the very same problem appears if we ask: How does a set of directions, directives, in a book (how does a poem, for example) know what *it* must become next in the course of becoming what in the end it has to be?

We are beginning, I am told, to know enough about the chromosome dance to have some promise of knowing more or less how it works. We may expect that we will know all we need to know about that long, long before we will know nearly enough about the dance of words—and the dances behind their dancing—to get any adequate answer to our questions: "How does a poem grow? How does it learn how to become itself? How does it know when it is finished?"

Incidentally, this way of formulating the question is not, I think, an instance of the Pathetic Fallacy. As soon as the notice of this talk went up, a friend greeted me with the remark: "You are a bold man to commit the Pathetic Fallacy in the title of a discussion!" But my title doesn't attribute anything to poems that they do not fully have. They are living, feeling, knowing *beings* in their own right; the so-called metaphor that treats a poem as organic is not a metaphor, but a literal description. A poem is an activity, seeking to become itself. All behavior (or activity, as I prefer to say: see *Speculative Instruments*, pp. 118–22) of organisms is organic.

But, of course, it must be *activity*. When we fall down-stairs that is not activity; going up them is.

This view that poems, books, views and so on, have some degree of self-responsibility—write their own tickets and pay for their own mistakes, and so on, can go too far. I remember Wittgenstein, soon after *Tractatus Logico-Philosophicus* was published, telling me there were two or three bad mistakes in it (not in the translation, he didn't complain about that, but in the thought). I innocently said: "Well, you can put in an errata slip and correct them in the second edition"—and found him staring at me as a Pillar of Society stares at a newly unmasked traitor: "How could I! It is my child! I could not murder it!" and so on.

Now to come a bit nearer to our specific question. Consider the word "father." How does it work? By a system of oppositions and collaborations with two other words: "mother" and "child."

I have chosen as evident an example as I can think of to illustrate mutual dependence of words on words. ("Center," "circumference," "circle" would be another example.) If I now add "husband," "wife," "family," we see, of course, that the mutual dependencies of words on words brought in by this change have now been immensely extended. We have jumped up from physiology to sociology, of course.

I have just used the words "of course." We all know, of course, that "of course" can be:

(1) a little gesture of modesty, a recognition of the audience's claim to intelligence;

(2) an aggressive warning: "Differ from me if you dare!";

(3) a self-comforting precaution against panic, or lots of other things besides, depending on the other words active (in the setting, in the then play of oppositions and collaborations) with "of course."

We could any of us go on indefinitely illustrating these oppositions and collaborations among words. All discourse illustrates them endlessly and inevitably. I would remind you here of two things:

(1) These collaborations and opposition within the channel have to do with:

(T) What is Talked of.

(S) What is Said about it.

(D) How Distant we are to T and S.

(V) How we Value ($+$ or $-$) $\dfrac{\text{T,S}}{\text{D}}$ (thus Distanced)

(A) The *so what?* How we would Adjust something to us, and/or Adjust ourselves to it as result of

(O) How we would Organize all this in the interest of

(P) The Purposive activity that is at the heart of the development, endeavouring to find and further itself in the poem. The collaborations and oppositions by which any utterance becomes whatever it is, and does what-

ever it does are the means
through which purpose pursues
itself.†

(2) The other thing I would remind you of is this:
language works not only by and through the words used
but through words not used. Indignant Ruskin observed
on one occasion, "I will not use the expressions which
occur to me." Poems in various ways are always doing
that. In poetry the rhyme-set, the alternates not adopted,
the "root-forming morphemes" (*Interpretation in
Teaching*, pp. 241–45) and so on through countless
varieties of possible interaction, allowed or precluded.
There is endless opposition and collaboration among
words that do not appear at all: shaping, modifying,
directing the activity of the growing poem at all points,
guiding it and helping it to find out what has to be, and
warning it when, if ever, it has become itself.‡

May I now be a little summary and dogmatic for
a moment? A vast, recent aberration of concern with
poets as subjects for biography has led too many to

† The diagram offered may be used as a *yantra:* In Hindu devo-
tional tradition, "yantra is a general term for instruments of worship,
namely, idols, pictures or geometrical diagrams. A yantra may serve
as . . . a kind of chart or schedule for the gradual evolution of a
vision." Heinrich Zimmer, *Myths and Symbols in Indian Art and
Civilization,* pages 140–41.

‡ See *Speculative Instruments,* Chapter II, "Towards a Theory
of Comprehending" for a fuller account of these functions, or jobs,
of language: *respects* or *dimensions* in which utterances may differ
from one another. It will be clear that this analysis is supplementary
to and not in conflict with such discussions as are offered in *Prac-
tical Criticism* in terms of Sense, Feeling, Tone, and Intention (pp.
180–88, 353–57).

think that poems just express items, incidents, occur-
rences, crises, and so on, in a poet's experience. And
here "experience" will mean *not* the imaginative, esem-
plastic activity of the growth of the poem, but some
excerpt from a poet's everyday living: what he saw, felt
or lived; what he did or what happened. I will not say
it is never so (or we would again be, probably, just
definition mongering) I will only say that we very
rarely can have the sort of evidence that would be
needed if we were really inquiring into this sort of
question.

The more usual thing—so far as available evidence
goes—is for a poem, as I began by saying, to form at
its inception a problem. The minimum problem I said
was the finding, or creation, of a situation—a confluence
of imaginative possibilities—able to support its growth.
The situation, that confluence of possibilities, is a sys-
tem of oppositions and collaborations among words. In
brief, a poem begins by creating a linguistic problem
whose solution by language will be the attainment of
its end.

To make the peculiarly *linguistic* character of this
problem more distinct let me contrast it explicitly both
with the biographical problems just mentioned and with
the literary or historical problems of a poem's genre or
of its relations to earlier poems. The contrasts hold, al-
though, and however much, all possible problems may,
in a given instance, be interconnected. The methods, the
concepts required, the direction and focus of attention
exacted, the standards that may be acceptable . . . differ

as we pass from one of these fields of perception and/or conjecture to another. Biographic speculations as to whatever in a poet's life shaped whatever in a poem must—at present, and very likely, always—have unassignable probabilities. Even when the poem *uses* verbal material, which is reported as having occurred in some biographically important incident, we would be rash to assume too confidently that the incident in any deep way determined the poem. Any sophisticated reader of good-quality detective fiction would smile at such naïve thinking in a Lestrade. The poem may just be using for its own purposes something that, in life, belonged in a different web. Yet biographic critics rarely show any such caution. The toils of their pursuit no doubt predispose them to overestimate their finds.

Comparative and historical studies, on the other hand, seem somewhat haunted by memories of burnt fingers. Early adventures in etymology, in folklore universalisms, in diffusionisms; examples from Frazer round to Freud seem to have had effect; humble pie has been widely served. The very elasticity of a genre has helped perhaps to discourage assertiveness. In brief, much scholarly reserve and mutual suspicion are to be observed.

Linguistic analysis, in contrast with both, mingles splash-happy recklessness with a methodological anxiety. Its dealing with archetypes, for example, range from one extreme to another. Bearing my title in mind, however, let me now look rather closely at a poem in which the mutual relevance of its parts—their oppositions and collaborations—seems rather more observable and describable than is usual. I hope thereby to bring out what one sort of linguistic account of the being of a poem may be like—not denying that there well may be other types of linguistic accounts and, still less, that biographic and literary-historical accounts may also be offered. Maybe the poet's correspondence, or notes preserved of his table talk, will enable some future biographer to write a very plausible short story about a possible process of composition for this poem. My point here is merely that, if so, it will be a short story to be placed properly in the genre detective fiction.

As a springboard in this, let me use a sentence from Northrop Frye. "The great writer seldom regards himself as a personality with something to say: his mind to him is simply a place where something happens to words." † This, as it stands, looks like a generalization from biographies; but that, I think, is largely a *façon de parler*. Language invites us continually to talk about poets under conditions which only entitle us to talk about poems. The substance of this sentence, for me, is that well-organized poems can be studied as places where transactions between words take place. Let us then consider how "something happens to words," without further regard for the poet, in the instance of William Empson's

† From his address "Humanities in a New World," Toronto, November 22, 1958. I wonder, who are *these* ?great? writers? How much can we know about them? Which of them has heretofore conceived of his mind so? Which could have?

LEGAL FICTION †

Law makes long spokes of the short stakes of men.
Your well fenced out real estate of mind
No high flat of the nomad citizen
Looks over, or train leaves behind.

5 Your rights extend under and above your claim
Without bound; you own land in Heaven and Hell;
Your part of earth's surface and mass the same,
Of all cosmos' volume, and all stars as well.

Your rights reach down where all owners meet, in Hell's
10 Pointed exclusive conclave, at earth's centre
(Your spun farm's root still on that axis dwells);
And up, through galaxies, a growing sector.

You are nomad yet; the lighthouse beam you own
Flashes, like Lucifer, through the firmament.
15 Earth's axis varies; your dark central cone
Wavers a candle's shadow, at the end.

A topic sentence; and then the rest of the poem an expansion, simultaneously literal and figurative. We need a diagram, which we can easily draw for ourselves.

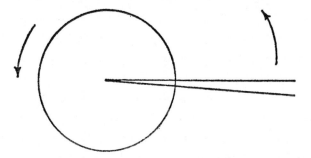

† From *Collected Poems of William Empson*, copyright, 1949, by William Empson. Reprinted by permission of Harcourt, Brace & World, Inc. and Chatto & Windus, Ltd.

short stakes: Both the stakes the prospector drives in to mark the boundaries of his claim (line 5) and the posts of the fence that keeps cattle (say) in and trespassers out of the spun farm (line 11). Rights in this land include everything under and above (line 5). They are *stakes*, too, in the sense in which a landowner is said to have a *stake* in the country. He has invested money, time and toil in his property; he has something *at stake*.

spokes: Because the earth rotates. (I am being thus explicit because in several classrooms I have met readers of high credentials who did not take this in.)

real estate of mind: The figurative meaning is being underlined: this is a state of mind and more, a set of mental acquisitions and developments, as much as it is a plot of earth. As such, its privacy is important.

No high flat (however much of a skyscraper penthouse apartment it may be) can command this. Its heights and its depths are quite beyond any such survey. Though the poem itself may seem to be attempting something of the sort, the fourth verse reaffirms what these third and fourth lines have asserted and adds indications as to why this is so, which are no small part of the completing movement.

nomad citizen: In contrast to the farmer (cultivating his garden). The fourth verse "comforts" this farmer, who may feel rather tied by his holding. He does a lot of travelling inevitably if his property is sweeping illimitably about in this fashion. It is a disturbing sort of comfort however: Lucifer is "fallen from

heaven" (Isaiah, 14:12) and the self itself is shad-
owed by itself, hidden from whatever light it may
produce.

you own land in Heaven and Hell: Both the conven-
tional Heaven (and Dante's Inferno) *and* all that
they betoken. Line 7 perhaps illustrates another sense
of "unfinished" from that with which we are con-
cerned: it seems to be in a rough, stop-gap, kind of
condition, but line 9 picks up again with

*where all owners meet, in Hell's/Pointed exclusive con-
clave:* A conclave is a locked-up place; specifically,
the cardinals electing a pope. Behind the geometrical
authority of the center (as determining the course
of any circumference) there may be "the grand con-
sult" of Milton's fallen Fiends as well as the uncom-
fortable communality of this joint possession—a high
price, indeed a confiscatory price, to pay for being
an owner.

What this sort of gloss should be attempting to
bring out is the dependence of what any word or
phrase can do in the poem upon what its other words
and phrases can do there: the degree of their mutual
enablement and mutual control. It is this—not any ac-
tions or agonies, and wishes or hopes or endeavors on
the part of the poet or his readers—that settles what
the poem may be and when and how (and whether)
it is finished. The problem the poem invents (or dis-
covers) is a linguistic problem in the sense that it is
solved (and there are many sorts as well as modes of

solution) through the collaborations of its constituent words. Any one reader, of course, is likely to enjoy, to participate in, but a portion of these. The same is true—as good poets have remarked—of the poet. It is arguable that in good poetry these collaborations among its words increase as the poem ages. The invention (or discovery) not only of the initial problem but of the derivative or resolving problems grows as, in imaginative study, what is happening in the poem relates itself to what has happened or could happen in other actual or possible poems. To compare poetry to a vastly simpler activity: a tennis player's game depends on other players.

The order of parts, temporal as well as implicational, within a poem may change greatly during composition. Quite often, I believe, the first phrase to occur—the phrase to which the rest of the poem is a response— becomes, in the final version, the close. To illustrate the varying ways in which parts of a poem may league with one another, and invite different spatio-temporal arrangements to favor one set of alliances rather than another, here is a poem of my own in two arrangements: on the left a form in which it settled down enough to get on galley proofs; on the right a different sequence which only Robert Lowell's arguments persuaded me to give it.

BY THE POOL†

In his meditation under the Bo tree, Gotama may have decided
—in love and pity—to teach a doctrine which would do men
good rather than another doctrine which few only could follow.

Not beneath the Bo tree
—Its long-tongued leaves
Poplar-like a-flutter—
This Buddha sits;
But by a limpid water
Welling by;

There search-winds of heaven
Twirl an imploring leaf,
Set the whole tree a-shiver
In glory, in grief:
Beneath, the All-giver
In pity willed
To bind up the Sheaf.

Which maybe more befits
Words none will utter
9 Whoever sigh.

Here by his River
That tumult's stilled.

10 There search-winds of heaven
Twirl an imploring leaf,
Set the whole tree a-shiver
In glory, in grief:
Beneath, the All-giver
In pity willed
To bind up the Sheaf.

Not ours to bind,
That way the sword;
Who lay aside the cord
They alone find.

Here by his River
That tumult's stilled.

Not beneath the Bo tree
—Its long-tongued leaves
Poplar-like a-flutter—
This Buddha sits;
But by a limpid water
Welling by;
Which maybe more befits
Words none will utter
Whoever sigh.

Truly inaudible
20 —Yet to be heard
By the ear of the mind—
The penultimate word,
Ultimate quibble:

Truly inaudible
—Yet to be heard
By the ear of the mind—
The penultimate word,

Not ours to bind,
That way the sword;

† From *The Screens and Other Poems*, © 1960, by I. A. Richards.
Reprinted by permission of Harcourt, Brace & World, Inc. and Rout-
ledge & Kegan Paul, Ltd.

Who lay aside the cord	Ultimate quibble.
They alone find.	
The still figure	The still figure
Beyond the flow	Beyond the flow
Listens, listened	Listens, listened
Aeons ago.	Aeons ago.
Ever a-flutter	Ever a-flutter
Must all words be.	Must all words be.
Here is an end.	Here is an end.

I presented the versions in parallel so to my audience in my talk with some remarks suggesting that the right-hand column should be regarded as a final form replacing an imperfect first draft printed on the left. This mode of treating the poem naturally put it on its mettle and, accordingly on the following day, it asserted its independence anew and reconstituted itself—reverting to the left hand version with these exceptions: lines 24–27 moved up to precede line 19, and in line 23 *ripple* replaced *quibble*.

Two remarks in conclusion: (1) The completion of a poem may be no matter of addition or excision, or of change in phrasing—though the change of one word may induce very extensive changes in the oppositions and collaborations among the other words. The completion may depend upon questions of sequence among parts otherwise seemingly invariant. Similarly, heightened attention to one word may lead to great changes in the mutual enablements of other words. Meter and rhyme are, of course, a poem's chief controls whereby words can be accorded attention or protected from it:

brought forward or distanced. (See D above.)

(2) Whatever the author may think himself entitled to do to a poem, the poem itself has the last word. It alone knows its duty. Authors, therefore, in their roles as critics, will be wise to pay particular attention to the dangers of misreading their own lines. The poem in its "persuasive continuity"—to use another phrase from Northrop Frye—is one thing. As frozen for critical examination it is different. The examining eye—the descriptive instrument or screen by which it is held stable for observation and appraisal—can and frequently does reform it. The proper moral to draw might be: *Let us not lose the poem in our account of it.* This might free the poem from much interference; but should not deprive it of any help afforded by light reflected from even mistaken critical opinions.

BIBLIOGRAPHY

BY I. A. RICHARDS

Coleridge on Imagination, ed. Kathleen Coburn, Bloomington, Ind., Indiana Univ. Press, 1960.

So Much Nearer: Essays Toward a World English, New York, Harcourt, Brace & World, 1968.

Design for Escape: World Education through Modern Media, New York, Harcourt, Brace & World, 1968.

How to Read a Page: A Course in Efficient Reading with an Introduction to 100 Great Words, New York, Norton, 1942.

(With C. K. Ogden) *The Meaning of Meaning*, New York, Harcourt, Brace & World, 1923, 1964.

Interpretation in Teaching, New York, Humanities Press, 1970.

Mencius on the Mind, New York, Humanities Press, 1932.

Practical Criticism, a Study of Literary Judgment, New York, Harcourt, Brace & World, 1935, 1968.

Principles of Literary Criticism, New York, Harcourt, Brace & World, 1925, 1968.

The Screens and Other Poems, New York, Harcourt, Brace & World; London, Routledge & Kegan Paul, Ltd., 1960.

Speculative Instruments, New York, Harcourt, Brace & World, 1967.

Why So, Socrates? a Dramatic Version, Cambridge, England, Cambridge Univ. Press, 1964.

Plato's Republic (ed.), Cambridge, England, Cambridge Univ. Press, 1967.